T0067011

CULTURE SMART!

CANADA

THE ESSENTIAL GUIDE TO
CUSTOMS & CULTURE

DIANE LEMIEUX AND
JULIANA TZVETKOVA

KUPERARD

"The real voyage of discovery consists not in seeking new landscapes, but in having new eyes."

Adapted from Marcel Proust, *Remembrance of Things Past.*

ISBN 978 1 78702 324 6

British Library Cataloguing in Publication Data
A CIP catalogue entry for this book is available
from the British Library

First published in Great Britain
by Kuperard, an imprint of Bravo Ltd
59 Hutton Grove, London N12 8DS
Tel: +44 (0) 20 8446 2440
www.culturesmart.co.uk
Inquiries: publicity@kuperard.co.uk

Design Bobby Birchall
Printed in Turkey

DIANE LEMIEUX was born in Quebec into a diplomatic family, and first moved abroad at the age of three. Her journey continued through eleven countries on five continents, during which she acquired four languages, two passports, and several cultural identities. She graduated with a B.A. in Communication from the University of Ottawa, an M.A. in Development Studies from Leeds University, a post-masters diploma in International Relations from the University of Amsterdam, and has a Journalism Diploma from Bath University. She started her career in international development, but decided more than twenty years ago to pursue her passion: writing. She is the author of four books, including *The Mobile Life: A New Approach to Moving Anywhere* and *Culture Smart! Nigeria.*

JULIANA TZVETKOVA is an academic and intercultural intelligence trainer. Born and educated in Bulgaria, she has an M.A. from Sofia University's Faculty of Classic and Modern Philology. After graduation she did translating, interpreting, and research, and worked for Bulgarian National Television. In 1998 Juliana moved with her family to Canada where she joined the Communications Faculty of Centennial College. She worked for Centennial around the globe for more than twenty years, and began her intercultural training career in Dubai. Today she combines her intercultural and educational work with writing. She has contributed to encyclopedias and is the author of *Pop Culture in Europe* and *Culture Smart! Bulgaria.*

CONTENTS

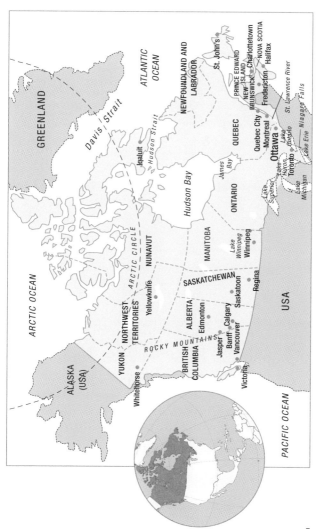

INTRODUCTION

Beyond its borders, Canada has long held a positive
reputation based on its international peacekeeping
activities, its stunning natural environment, and the
modest and understated nature of its people. The
idea that the French-speaking part would want to
split from such a wonderful place is confounding
to most outsiders. Beyond that, people assume that
Canadians are culturally similar to, though perhaps
more humble than, their American neighbors to
the south.

But Canada is a far more complex society than
the world's news media might lead you to believe.
In the past decades, Canada has become distinctly
multicultural: its small population is spread across
a vast territory, which affects how Canadians
communicate with each other. Politically and
economically the country is very decentralized, a
fact that affects the way business is done: Canadians
trade far more with the rest of the world than they
do interprovincially.

Canada is one of the world's wealthiest nations,
with one of the largest economies and a quality of
life among the best in the world. Though Canadians
remain proud of their nationality, events of the
past decade have challenged their sense of national
identity as well as their reputation abroad: climate
change, the Covid-19 pandemic, the treatment

of its indigenous population, its handling of the anti-vax "freedom convoy," and the dramatic natural disasters of 2021 are events that are shaping Canadian society in the twenty-first century.

Culture Smart! Canada gives a broad overview of the geography, history, and politics of the country, and describes the Canadians themselves, their values, attitudes, and the routine of their daily lives. It looks at how Canadians use their spare time, and how you can make friends with them. There is a chapter on traveling within the country, and another on business for those who need to know what to expect in the corporate world—for instance, the specific rules of etiquette at business meetings, and how Canadians negotiate deals.

A book of this size cannot hope to do full justice to the rich cultural variety that exists within the country, yet it aims to guide you through the complexities of the Canadian psyche and so prepare you for the reactions, emotions, and events that you are likely to experience during your visit. Canadians are open, friendly, and relaxed hosts, who will make your stay worthwhile, and will welcome you even more if you can demonstrate some depth of knowledge of their culture.

Official Name	Canada	
Capital City	Ottawa	In Ontario
Main Cities and Towns	Victoria, Vancouver, Calgary, Edmonton, Regina, Winnipeg, Toronto, Quebec City, Montreal, Fredericton, Halifax, Charlottetown, St. John's, White Horse, Yellowknife, Iqualuit	
Area	3,855,106 sq. miles (9,984,670 sq. km)	Includes 10 provinces and 3 territories
Terrain	Varies widely across the country. Includes tundra, flat plains, mountains, vast forests, lakes, and rivers	
Climate	Continental climate: cold winters and warm summers	Regional variations include cold northern regions, a wet and mild west coast, and a snowy east coast.
Currency	The Canadian Dollar	CAD, or Can$
Population	38.7 million (approx.)	
Ethnic Makeup	About 73% are of European descent. About 13.6% are of French descent; 4.9% Indigenous.	The rest come from all other areas of the world. Approx. 21.5% of the population is foreign born.
National Languages	The official languages are English and French; 18% speak at least 2 languages.	About 75% are native English speakers; 21.4% are native French speakers. 200 languages are reported as home or native languages.
Religion	Around 63.2% are Christian; 26.3% claim no religious affiliation.	The remaining 10.5% are Buddhist, Hindu, Jewish, Muslim, Sikh, or other.

Government	Constitutional monarchy, still linked to the British Crown	Bicameral parliament at both federal and provincial levels. The federal executive is headed by the prime minister.
Media	National public network providers CBC, SRC, CTV, and Global/Can West. Several commercial networks, regional and local networks. Cable and satellite TV broadly available	National papers: *The Globe and Mail*, *National Post* (English); *La Presse*, *Le Devoir* (French). Also many provincial and municipal papers
Electricity	120 volts, 60 Hz	
Economy	Highly developed mixed-market economy	Main exports include crude oil, cars, gold, wood, coal, fertilizer, wheat, and aluminium.
Internet Domain	.ca	
Telephone	Canada's country code is 1.	Each province has its own 3-digit code. To dial out of Canada, dial 011.
Time Zones	There are six time zones across Canada. From east to west they are: Newfoundland Time: GMT minus 3.5 hrs Atlantic Time: GMT minus 4 hrs Eastern Time: GMT minus 5 hrs Central Time: GMT minus 6 hrs Mountain Time: GMT minus 7 hrs Pacific Time: GMT minus 8 hrs	

CHAPTER ONE

LAND & PEOPLE

Canada is the second oldest federal democracy in the world. It is also one of the most multicultural societies on earth due to a high level of immigration that continues to affect the makeup of its people. Its history and geography have profoundly influenced the way Canadians live and think.

A mari usque ad mare
(From sea to sea)
Motto of Canada

GEOGRAPHICAL SNAPSHOT

The Canadian psyche is deeply influenced by the vast size of its territory and the extremes of its climate. Canada is the second-largest country in the world, in total area, after Russia. It is also the second-most sparsely populated country in the world, after Australia. It stretches from the Atlantic Ocean in the

The Battery, a neighborhood on the slopes of Signal Hill at the entry to the harbor of the historic city of St. John's, Newfoundland.

east to the Pacific Ocean in the west, spanning six time zones. To the north is the Arctic Ocean and to the south are 5,592 miles (9,000 km) of uninterrupted border with the United States. From coast to coast there are vast forests, breathtaking mountains, flat, open plains, and thousands of lakes and rivers. In terms of fresh water, Canada is the richest country in the world.

Six Geographic Regions

The eastern coast is known as the Appalachian region. It includes the provinces of Newfoundland and Labrador, Prince Edward Island, New Brunswick, and Nova Scotia, as well as a part of Quebec south of the St. Lawrence River known as the Gaspé Peninsula. The region is mainly forested, hilly, and sparsely populated.

The mighty Niagara Falls. In the background, spanning the Niagara River gorge, is the Rainbow Bridge, which connects Canada and the USA.

Moving from east to west, the Great Lakes and St. Lawrence Lowlands region corresponds to the southern half of the provinces of Ontario and Quebec. This area is home to more than half of Canada's population and is an important agricultural and manufacturing center. This is where most of the country's largest cities are found. It is also home to the Niagara Falls and the Great Lakes, which form the largest group of freshwater lakes in the world and contain 20 percent of the planet's fresh surface water.

Still further west are the interior (or Great) Plains. This region runs through the provinces of Manitoba, Saskatchewan, and Alberta. Once vast plains, the region is now Canada's wheat basket and largest source of petroleum and natural gas.

The magnificent Emerald Lake in the Canadian Rockies. Yoho National Park, British Columbia.

The fourth region is the Western Cordillera, which straddles Alberta and British Columbia, making its way up through the Yukon Territory. Here, the Rocky Mountains provide a top-quality, four-season tourist attraction for nature and sports enthusiasts.

To the north there are two geographic regions: the Canadian Shield and the Arctic Archipelago. The Canadian Shield, stretching across northern Quebec, Ontario, and Manitoba, is a wild, remote area covered with forests and dotted with lakes and rivers. The land in the arctic region, where no trees grow because of the cold and dry temperatures, is known as tundra, where the top layer of soil is permafrost—it is frozen all year round.

CLIMATE

It is a myth that it is always cold in Canada. In fact, the seasonal (and daily) variation in weather conditions is probably one reason why the weather is the favorite topic of conversation across the country. It is unpredictable, quirky, sometimes extreme, and never "just right."

Roughly speaking, the warmest temperatures across the country are found in the south along the border with the USA. This is also, incidentally, the area where most Canadians live. From east to west, the eastern provinces get the most snow in the winter and have the coolest summers; the prairies get the coldest winters; British Columbia has the mildest summers and the mildest winters, but the highest humidity and rainfall.

One of the pleasures of the Canadian climate is the seasonal variety; visually, emotionally, and in terms of one's wardrobe, it creates a feeling of constant renewal and change.

Summers everywhere are generally warm and pleasant. The warmest regions are in the southern areas of British Columbia (for instance, in Vancouver), and in southern Ontario. Every year usually brings a few weeks of hot weather of around 86°F (30°C). This can be unpleasant in Toronto, where the humidity makes the city muggy and sticky. Evenings everywhere are generally cool, making warm sweaters essential if you plan to be out of doors.

Fall is a particularly beautiful time in Canada, when the leaves of the maple trees change color, turning the

SOME CANADIAN WINTER WORDS

- **Blizzard:** a snowstorm with heavy snowfall, high winds, low visibility, and temperatures below 14°F (−10°C).
- **Ice storm:** freezing rain that coats everything, including roads, trees, and power lines, with a thin layer of ice. Temperatures hover around 32°F (0°C).
- **Cold snap:** when temperatures drop 25 degrees or more within eighteen hours. Warnings on the radio and TV will remind people to cover their skin, nose, and mouth completely if they really must go outside.
- **Chinook:** a warm, dry, westerly wind that blows in the winter off the Rocky Mountains and onto the Great Plains. It can raise the temperature by 36°F (20°C) in fifteen minutes.
- **Snow tires,** or **all-season radials:** specially designed tires that are a "must have" on Canada's winter roads.
- **Traction mats:** what you put under your wheels to get your car moving when it gets stuck in the snow.
- **Galoshes,** or **rubbers:** rubber overshoes that protect your fine leather shoes from the snow and salt on the winter roads.
- **Skidoo boots:** boots with an inner shell and an outer, plasticized shell. They all look exactly alike, and are clumpy and hard to put on, but every Canadian child wears them.
- **Tuque:** a knitted hat that keeps your ears warm.

countryside, particularly in the eastern St. Lawrence area, into a painter's paradise. There is a crisp freshness in the air, and a sense of busy preparation for the long months of hibernation to come.

Canadian winters are long, and the further north you go, the longer, colder, and darker they get. Even along the southernmost band of the country, winter temperatures are usually below 32°F (0°C). In Yellowknife the average winter temperature is –18.4°F (–28°C), and in Toronto it is 19.4°F (–7°C). Every winter has its cold streak for a week or more, with temperatures of 0°F (–18°C) or colder. Snowfall, particularly east of Toronto, can be very heavy—an irritant for car drivers but a bonanza for outdoor sports enthusiasts.

And after a long winter, spring is wet and muddy, but the explosion of nature's renewal puts everyone in a good mood.

THE PEOPLE

There are approximately 38.7 million Canadians living in almost 3.85 million square miles (almost 10 million sq. km) of territory. Of course, people are not all spread out evenly over the whole country: 81 percent of the population live in urban centers, and more than 75 percent live within a hundred miles (160 km) of the border with the United States. But people who live in St. John's, Newfoundland, are 3,135 miles

Inuit mother and child in the Qikiqtaaluk region, Nunavut.

(5,045 km) from those living in Vancouver—considerably farther away than people who live in London are from those in Tehran—2,738 miles (4,406 km).

There is also the country's diversity in terms of "cultures of origin." Indigenous Canadians (4.9 percent of the total population), include the First Nations, Métis, and Inuit peoples. European immigration began with the French and British, primarily to work in the agricultural or rural extractive industries. In the late nineteenth century, successive waves of immigrants arrived, first from Eastern Europe and China. After the Second World War immigration expanded increasingly, in response to needs in the manufacturing, infrastructure, and construction sectors. Today, Canada has one of the highest per capita immigration rates in the world, creating a population of more than two hundred and fifty ethnic groups. More than one in five Canadians are foreign-born.

Language and Identity

There are two official languages in most of Canada: English and French. In the three northern territories indigenous languages are also officially recognized.

According to the 2021 census, native English speakers, known as Anglophones, make up around 75 percent of the population; native French speakers, Francophones, are 21.4 percent. The remaining Canadians are Allophones whose mother tongue is neither French nor English.

Despite the existence of two official languages, only around 18 percent of Canadians are bilingual (native French speakers are more likely to speak English than the other way round). The first Canadian Official Languages Act was passed in 1969 and requires government institutions to provide federal services in both languages across the country. New Brunswick is the only officially bilingual province where provincial public services are also provided in both languages. It is true that all product labels are bilingual across the country (this falls under federal legislation). Many Canadians claim that their most effective source of bilingual education was reading the cereal boxes at breakfast time.

However, bilingualism with a language other than French or English is increasingly common: in the 2021 census, more than 200 languages were reported as home languages. There are eleven indigenous language groups that include more than sixty-five distinct languages and dialects. But the country's biggest source of linguistic diversity is through immigration. Chinese languages are the third-most common mother tongue, spoken by almost 3 percent of the total population. Other common language groups are Indo-Iranian, Slavic, and Romance languages. Cree, Inuktitut, and Ojibwemowin are the most commonly spoken indigenous languages.

A BRIEF HISTORY

Canada is a relatively young nation that is still evolving in terms of its cultural makeup. Its development has largely been defined by immigration, the exploitation of its natural resources, and the forging of an identity in the shadow of its large southern neighbor, the United States of America.

The First Peoples

The first inhabitants of Canada arrived around fifteen thousand years ago over the Bering Strait from Asia. As they spread out over the vast territory, they gradually developed several language groups, sophisticated customs, values, beliefs, laws, and systems of government. These First Nations peoples had historical and political relationships through which they traded or fought. Their world was rich and complex. And then came the Europeans.

The Viking explorer Leif Eriksson probably reached the east coast of Canada around 1,000 CE and

Pîhtokahanapiwiyin, the Plains Cree chief also known as Poundmaker, and his wife, c. 1884.

established a settlement, which was later abandoned. However, the real impact of white Europeans began with the "discovery" of Canada in 1497 by John Cabot, an Italian explorer in the service of Henry VII of England. During this period, the Spanish, French, British, and Italians fought to expand their dominion over the "new world." In 1534 Jacques Cartier, a Frenchman sailing under commission from François I, reached the gulf of the St. Lawrence River and claimed the surrounding area for France.

The Name

Canada's name originates from the early exploratory visits by Jacques Cartier in 1534. It is derived from *kanata*, a Huron–Algonquin word for "village."

Initial contact with Europeans in eastern Canada brought diseases that wiped out entire villages. However, through the growth of the fur trade, mainly peaceful relationships were established between the white man and the Native Peoples of Canada.

The English–French competition for dominance in the fur trade was superimposed over an age-old Iroquois–Algonquin antagonism that eventually led to the English-supported Iroquois wars against the French and their Huron–Algonquin allies.

Though the history of European settlement in Canada is less violent than in the rest of the Americas, colonial territorial expansion eventually ended the traditional way of life of the Native Peoples. The Indian Act of 1876 imposed a colonial system of governance on First Nations communities that gave authority to the federal government. Only in 1982 did the Constitution Act recognize the inherent right of the indigenous peoples to self-government. This led, from 1995, to the negotiation of self-government agreements. Today, twenty-five self-government agreements involving forty-three indigenous communities have been signed. More than fifty agreements are still being negotiated.

The Colonies

The first permanent European settlement in Canada was established by the French explorer Samuel de Champlain in 1608 at Stadacona, the Iroquois village that was to become Quebec City. French expansion of their colony was fueled in the first instance by a desire to gain and maintain a monopoly in the fur trade. It was also driven by the missionary zeal of the Roman Catholic Church to accumulate souls.

The first agricultural settlement in the new territories was in what is now Nova Scotia. These French settlers became known as Acadians. They were isolated from the Quebecois settlers for long enough to form a separate Francophone identity, which is still strong today.

It was only in the second half of the 1600s that the government in France realized the need to provide the colony with a rational and effective local government similar to the administrative structures in place in the English colonies to the south.

During this period, the British established the Hudson's Bay Company. Two Frenchmen, Radisson and des Groseilliers, saw the possibilities of a lucrative fur trade in the northern interior. Their request for resources to establish a trading network was rejected by potential French financiers, and they turned instead to their English competitors. In May 1670 a Royal Charter granted the lands of the Hudson Bay watershed to the "Governor and Company Adventurers of England trading into Hudson Bay." The company began with forts and trading posts around the James and Hudson

Bays, gradually expanding westward to control huge tracts of land across northern and central Canada.

INDIGENOUS PEOPLES OFFICIALLY RECOGNIZED IN CANADA

There are three separate groups of indigenous people in Canada. These statistics reflect the numbers of people self-identifying as members of one of the following groups.

- The Inuit people live in the northernmost regions of Canada. The term "Eskimo" is no longer used, at their request. They are estimated at 65,025 people.
- The Métis are the descendants of French fur traders and native women in what is now Manitoba. They speak Michif, a mix of French and Cree. The Métis developed a distinctive culture and think of themselves as a nation. Their numbers are currently estimated at around 587,545.
- "First Nations" regroups all other indigenous tribes in Canada, totaling approximately 977,230.

Together, there are more than 1.67 million people, 4.9 percent of the total population, who identify themselves as Native Peoples.

> **Did You Know?**
> The Hudson's Bay Company is one of the world's oldest commercial corporations. At its peak, it was the world's largest private landowner, and functioned as the de facto government of British-controlled Canada for several centuries. Its network of trading posts formed the basis for present-day cities and towns in much of western Canada.

In 1745, a British force moved up from New England and captured the fort of Louisbourg in Nova Scotia, giving the British control over a large French-speaking Acadian population. Ten years after their victory, they deported more than twelve thousand Acadians in what is known as the Great Expulsion. In a period of eight years they were shipped out to the four corners of the planet, separating families and destroying lives. Around four thousand eventually made it to Louisiana, where they became known as Cajuns; a large group returned to the Atlantic Provinces, where their Acadian roots continue to flourish.

The year 1759 was a decisive one in the balance of power between the French and English in Canada. The Battle of the Plains of Abraham, which took place outside the walls of Quebec City, pitted the army of General Montcalm of France against the British forces led by General Wolfe. Montcalm's defeat spelled the loss of French control over Quebec and the St. Lawrence.

The Death of General Wolfe, by Benjamin West, 1770.

Within four years the entire region that would become eastern Canada was ceded to Great Britain.

In the increasing tensions building up to the war of independence in the United States, the British sought to create stability in their Canadian colonies and build French-Canadian loyalty to the Crown. The demands of the French-speaking population of Quebec were addressed in the Quebec Act of 1774. This gave French Canadians the rights to practice their Roman Catholic religion and to retain their language and the use of the French Civil Code. It also confirmed the semi-feudal system of land ownership called *seigneuries*. However, there was no elected legislative assembly; the province was managed by a governor and a legislative council appointed by the British Crown. Despite the limited degree of political independence it represented, the Act was a vital turning point in the development of the Canadian nation, in that it recognized the cultural differences between its French and English subjects—a concept that was a radical departure for the period.

Under the Seigneurial land ownership system, the land belonged to the king of France and was maintained by the landlord (*seigneur*). The system remained relatively intact for another hundred years and was formally abolished in 1854, though some aspects of it continued into the twentieth century, when the last feudal land bonds were repurchased through provincial bonds.

Large numbers of Loyalists fled to Canada after American independence. They settled particularly in the areas south of the St. Lawrence River, known as the Eastern Townships. These individuals had lost everything fighting for the British Crown

Portrait of the Mohawk leader Thayendanegea ("Joseph Brant"), by George Romney, 1776.

during the war, and loudly claimed their right to land ownership. Under the Quebec Act, however, they were not entitled to own land in the province because of the Seigneurial system. Britain did not want to lose control over Canada as it had the United States, and the interests of the Loyalists across the country were taken seriously.

In 1791 the Constitutional Act split Quebec into Upper Canada (Ontario) and Quebec (Lower Canada). Each was governed by a legislative council appointed for life and a legislative assembly that was elected by the people. In practice, however, power lay with the Governor appointed by the British government and his executive advisors. In 1837, John George Lambton, Earl of Durham, presented the *Report on the Affairs of British North America*. The report suggested that the provinces be merged under one legislature and given the right of self-governance, which would make them more, rather than less, loyal to the British Crown. This process was accomplished in the 1840 Act of the Union.

During this period, skirmishes continued in the west between the Americans and the British. The War of 1812—fought in part over British violation of US maritime rights, against the backdrop of the struggle between Britain and Napoleonic France—effectively ended in a draw. This was the last war between Canada and the USA, and protracted negotiations in Ghent culminated in 1814 in the restoration of the status quo and the drawing of the current border.

Peace with the USA. *The Signing of the Treaty of Ghent, Christmas Eve, 1814*, by Amédée Forestier.

The Birth of a Nation: Not Revolution, But Devolution

In 1867 the Constitution Act (formerly known as the British North America Act) established the Dominion of Canada, which at that time consisted of Ontario, Quebec, Nova Scotia, and New Brunswick. While none of the agreements of the 1774 Quebec Act were revoked, it transformed the government of all the Canadian provinces to the legislative assembly system, basically as it exists today (see the section on the government structure below). One year later the Rupert's Land Act transferred ownership of the immense territory owned by the Hudson's Bay Company to the union. This vast area was later divided into the province of Manitoba and the Northwest Territories.

By 1885, the Canadian west was physically connected to the rest of the country with the official opening of the transcontinental railroad. By 1912 all of the provinces and territories had joined the Federation except Newfoundland and Labrador, which joined in 1949. The last territorial change occurred in 1992 when the residents of the Northwest Territories voted to split the region roughly along ethnic lines, creating the Dene region of the Northwest Territories and the Inuit region of Nunavut in the northeast.

The Twentieth Century

The first large wave of European immigration to Canada in the early twentieth century (mainly from the British Isles, Russia, and Eastern Europe, along with small numbers from around the world) took place before the First World War, increasing its population, particularly in the western regions, and diversifying its cultural mix. Canada automatically joined the war on the side of the British and, to the bitter disagreement of the French Canadians, established a compulsory military draft. In 1931, the Statute of Westminster affirmed Canada's independence as a self-governing country within the Commonwealth of Nations.

The Great Depression of the 1930s hit Canadians hard; tens of thousands of people became dependent

Lantern slide of the interior of a settler's house made some time before 1911.

on government relief or charity, leading to social chaos and economic stagnation. The role and size of the government increased as it stepped in to take more control over the economy, such as by establishing the Bank of Canada to regulate monetary policy, and introducing social measures such as credit schemes and aid programs. The events of this decade were a key element in the development of the welfare system that exists today.

During the Second World War, Canada's parliament approved the country's active participation. The Canadian economy boomed as a consequence of the war effort, boosting the development of the

Recruitment poster by Henry Eveleigh, 1942.

manufacturing sector and establishing Canada's position in international trade relations. Former Prime Minister Lester B. Pearson won a Nobel Peace Prize in 1957 for creating the UN's first designated peacekeeping mission and helping to avert war over the Suez Canal. Its refusal to participate in the Vietnam War (1964–1973) further cemented Canada's reputation for international moderation and peacekeeping. The postwar years saw another massive wave of European immigration and a steady increase in prosperity across the country.

In the second half of the century, a "Quiet Revolution" swept across Quebec. A wide gap had existed between the social and economic standing of the French-speaking population of Quebec—under the thumb of the Catholic Church, which ran most schools and supported an agrarian, anti-business policy—and the rest of the country. Starting in the 1960s, French Canadian society rapidly became secularized; church attendance dropped suddenly, and massive investments in public education and social welfare systems stimulated the participation of the Quebecois in their province's economic development.

GOVERNMENT

Canada is a constitutional monarchy—the King of England is also the King of Canada, a purely symbolic figurehead. He is represented in Canada by the Governor General, who is appointed by him on the advice of the Canadian prime minister.

Federal (National) Government

The national government is composed of the head of state (the King), the elected House of Commons (the lower house), and the appointed Senate (the upper house). The Senate is supposed to be the house of review for legislation but is largely a rubber stamp for the lower house. There is a general agreement on the need to reform the almost toothless Senate, and some would like to see it either abolished altogether or its members elected.

Real power lies with Canada's 308-seat parliament. Canadians don't vote for their prime minister directly; they elect a member of parliament in their "riding," or electoral district. The candidate with the most votes wins (they don't need an absolute majority). The leader of the party with the most seats becomes

The Canadian Parliament in Ottawa.

prime minister. He or she (the Right Honorable Kim Campbell was the first and, until now, the only female prime minister of Canada, in 1993) usually forms a cabinet from the members of his or her party who were elected to the House of Commons. A government is normally elected for a four-year period, which can be extended to a fifth year. In reality, the decision to hold elections rests solely with the prime minister, and Canadians have gone back to the polls after much shorter periods. A government can also be defeated by a vote of the House of Commons on a matter of confidence, such as a vote on the budget.

In 2022 there were six main political parties in parliament: the Conservative Party, the Liberal Party, the New Democratic Party, the Bloc Québécois, the Green Party, and the Forces et Démocracie party. Only the first two parties have ever gained enough votes across the country to form a government. Power is shared with the provincial authorities.

FEDERAL GOVERNMENT RESPONSIBILITIES

National defense	Criminal law
Employment insurance	Postal services
Census	Fisheries
Trade regulation	Foreign affairs
Banking and federal taxes	Shipping, railways, telephones, and pipelines
Citizenship	Indigenous lands and rights

PROVINCIAL GOVERNMENT RESPONSIBILITIES

Property and civil rights	Administration of justice
Natural resources and the environment	Education
Health	Welfare

PROVINCES AND TERRITORIES

The federal capital is Ottawa, in the province of Ontario.

The ten provinces are, from west to east:

Province	Capital City
British Columbia	Victoria
Alberta	Edmonton
Saskatchewan	Regina
Manitoba	Winnipeg
Ontario	Toronto
Quebec	Quebec City
New Brunswick	Fredericton
Nova Scotia	Halifax
Prince Edward Island	Charlottetown
Newfoundland and Labrador	St. John's

The three territories are:

Yukon	Whitehorse
Northwest Territories	Yellowknife
Nunavut	Iqaluit

Provinces and Territories

The next level of government is provincial and territorial. Here the structure is quite similar to the federal system, with a Lieutenant Governor representing the Governor General. Elections are held every four or five years (except in British Columbia, where they have fixed-date elections every four years on the second Tuesday in May) and the leader of the largest party becomes the premier in the provincial or territorial legislature. There is no Senate at this level.

One of the cornerstones of this federal–provincial balancing act is the "transfer payments" from the federal government to the provinces and territories. There are two types of payment. Equalization Payments go to poorer regions to compensate for their smaller revenue base. These payments aim to balance the standard of living between Canada's regions. Program Payments are divided into Health Transfer Payments and Social Transfer Payments (which include responsibilities such as higher education, social assistance, and child welfare). These payments are made in order to support programs that the federal government deems important but for which it has no provincial jurisdiction. The catch, from the perspective of the provinces, is that the federal government can attach conditions to these payments that effectively cramp provincial authority.

Balance of Power

The spice in Canadian politics comes with the struggle for power between the federal and provincial/territorial legislatures. In broad terms, the federal government is responsible for issues that affect all Canadians, such as defense, foreign policy, and citizenship. The provincial governments are responsible for areas such as education, health, and roads. Some sectors are shared. For instance, there are federal and provincial ministries of the environment

QUEBEC'S INDEPENDENCE MOVEMENT

Tension between the Francophone, Catholic people of Quebec and the mostly Anglophone, Protestant population of the rest of Canada has been present since the early beginnings of the Canadian nation.

Sovereigntists, also referred to as separatists, believe that the Quebec government does not have the constitutional power to act in the province's best social, political, and economic interests. Independentist sentiment has brought the ire of people in the rest of the country and disbelief from the rest of the world.

In 1967 General de Gaulle, France's president at that time, visited the province of Quebec during Montreal's World's Fair. In a speech from the balcony of City Hall, he fueled the fire of a nascent political nationalism with the words "*Vivre le Québec Libre!*" ("Long live a free Quebec!"). In 1970, the Front de Libération du Québec (FLQ) kidnapped and killed the deputy premier of the province, Pierre Laporte. The prime minister of Canada, Pierre Trudeau, declared martial law in Quebec and jailed separatist sympathizers, a period of time known as the October Crisis. These actions were well received in the rest of the country, but only served to fuel separatist sentiment in the province.

In 1976, an openly separatist provincial government was voted into power, led by René Lévesque. He oversaw, in 1980, a referendum on sovereignty for Quebec, which was rejected by a solid majority in the province. In 1995, a similar referendum was held; this time independence was rejected by a margin of less than 1 percent of the province's population.

After the constitutional negotiations of 1987 and 1992, separatist sentiment in the twenty-first century has been marked by "separation fatigue." Though the status of Quebec within the union is regarded as an unresolved issue by many, a 2020 survey (twenty-five years after the referendum) reported that, if polled today, only 36 percent of the population would vote "yes" to leave the union. It is probably safe to say that Quebec is more confident today about its own identity and place within the Canadian polity than at any other time in its history.

and shared responsibilities in telecommunications and transportation.

In 1982, the Canada Act "patriated" the constitution to enable the Canadian government to make constitutional changes. The Act also added a Charter of Rights and Freedoms to the constitution, enshrined a commitment to fiscal equalization among the provinces, and expanded provincial jurisdiction over natural resources. The new constitution was eventually adopted but signed by only ten of Canada's eleven first ministers: Quebec did not sign because it was not officially recognized as a "distinct society." The bitter negotiations eroded trust between the provinces as well as between the provincial and federal levels of government.

In 1987, the then prime minister, Brian Mulroney, negotiated constitutional modifications with the provincial premiers. Known as the Meech Lake Accord, the agreement would have increased the powers of the provincial governments in certain spheres and, importantly, recognized the province of Quebec as a distinct society. The accord required the consent of all provincial and federal legislatures within three years. After more bitter negotiations, two provinces (Newfoundland and Labrador, and Manitoba) refused to sign, largely because of the anti-Quebec sentiments it unleashed.

In 1992, the Charlottetown Accords were a second attempt at constitutional reform. The package addressed many longstanding disputes around the division of powers between the federal and provincial jurisdictions. This accord was decided by national referendum and was also defeated. Today, the division of legislative powers and responsibilities between the federal and provincial governments remain as enshrined in the Constitution Act of 1867 and continue to be a source of legal debate and political dispute.

Hay bales on the Canadian prairies. Alberta, Saskatchewan, and Manitoba are major grain producers.

THE ECONOMY

Canada is the ninth-largest economy in the world, has one of the highest levels of economic freedom, and is among the world's wealthiest nations. Its market economy is tempered by social security and universal health care systems that provide a nationwide safety net, though the most recent statistics indicate that 6.4 percent of the population live in poverty.

Canada weathered the 2008 debt crisis well and by early 2020 (before the onset of the Covid-19 pandemic) it had a strong balance sheet, the lowest net debt-to-GDP ratio in the G7, and historically low borrowing rates. Income inequality, already on the decrease since 2015, shrank significantly due in large part to pandemic support programs.

Hydroelectric power being generated at the Sir Adam Beck Generating Complex, Niagara Falls.

Its modern economy is dominated by the service industry, where three-quarters of all Canadians find employment. It has a sizable manufacturing sector, particularly in Ontario. However, Canada is unique among developed countries in the importance of its natural resource sector, which accounts for nearly 60 percent of the country's exports. Major industries are logging, agriculture, and mining, as well as commercial fishing and seafood. It is one of the world's top three exporters of wheat and is the world's leading producer of zinc and uranium.

Canada is also a net exporter of energy, with large oil and gas reserves in the east and west, and abundant hydroelectric power in several provinces, particularly in Quebec. Energy makes up nearly 10 percent of Canada's total GDP and more than a fifth of its total exports.

The Canadian economy is highly dependent on trade, leaving it open to market fluctuations in commodity prices. While the economy shrank in 2020 (–5.2 percent) as a result of the pandemic, the GDP growth rate was a solid 5.7 percent in 2021, with an unemployment rate of 7.5 percent (down from 9.6 percent in 2020). In 2022, Canada was battling the impact of the war in the Ukraine, the cost of the pandemic, and numerous natural disasters (forest fires and flooding).

Given the length of the border between the two countries, it is not surprising that Canada and the United States are the world's largest trading partners. The 1989 Free Trade Agreement and 1994 North American Free Trade Agreement (with Mexico) and the 2020 revision of NAFTA, the United States–Mexico–Canada Agreement, increased trade dramatically: in 2022 Canada and the USA traded US $2 billion in goods and services daily.

Regionalism

What surprises many visitors is the level of internal (provincial) barriers to trade that are a part of the daily reality in Canada. For example, provinces and territories restrict cross-border purchases of alcohol; technical, sector-specific regulations can differ across provinces and territories, such as vehicle weight standards; and regulatory and administrative rules create bureaucratic hurdles. There are, in fact, fewer barriers of this sort between the countries of the European Union than between the provinces and territories of Canada.

Other examples of nontariff barriers are those that affect labor mobility. For certain occupations or trades— such as teachers, doctors, nurses, engineers, architects, electricians, plumbers, and car mechanics—there are residency requirements, licenses, or certification requirements (which are valid generally only in one province or territory), or different standards that make working in another province or territory difficult, time-consuming to arrange, or expensive.

The 2017 Canadian Free Trade Agreement sought to strengthen and modernize internal trade relations; internal trade is currently estimated to contribute only one-fifth of Canada's GDP.

THE LEGAL SYSTEMS

Canada's judiciary acts much as in other developed countries. It is independent and has the power to strike down laws that go against the constitution. The Supreme Court of Canada is the highest court and final arbiter.

What is unique to Canada is that there are officially two legal systems in the country. Common law is used everywhere except in Quebec, where the French Civil Code is practiced.

Law enforcement falls under provincial jurisdiction, although most policing in the country is done by the Royal Canadian Mounted Police (RCMP). They are the federal police force, enforcing national law. However, all of the territories and most of the provinces subcontract policing to the RCMP, particularly in rural areas. Some municipal police forces are also RCMP-contracted. The Ontario Provincial Police, the Sûreté du Québec, and the Royal Newfoundland Constabulary are independent provincial forces.

CANADA IN THE WORLD

Canada generally scores highly in international comparison tables such as the United Nation's Human Development Index. It is a founding member of both the United Nations and the North Atlantic Treaty Organization (NATO), is a member of the Organization of American States (OAS), and participates in military operations that are sanctioned by the UN and in NATO operations. In terms of economic power, it is a member of the Organization for Economic Cooperation and Development (OECD) and the Group of Seven (G7).

Prime Minister Trudeau has striven to make Canada a leading exponent of liberal values, an effort that has led his opponents to criticize his "wokeness." For example, he has ensured gender parity (fifteen women and fifteen men) in his cabinets ever since his first election to office in 2015, and has sought to achieve a more diverse representation that better reflects the Canadian population. In 2016 the government legalized assisted dying. In 2018, cannabis was decriminalized across the country, making Canada just the second country in the world to legalize recreational use of the drug. Since then

Tribute in Regina, Saskatchewan, to the Indigenous children who died in state-funded institutions.

cannabis is estimated to have added more than Can$40 billion and over 150,000 jobs to the economy.

However, in recent years Canada has come to the world's attention for other reasons. In May 2021, the first reports emerged of the discovery of the remains of 200 Indigenous children in an unmarked grave at a former residential school. This was the first of several such discoveries at church-run, government-funded institutions around the country that were established essentially to eradicate indigenous cultures and languages. The findings shocked Canadians and the world, even though a 2015 report had already indicated that at least 4,000 students had died at these schools, which existed from the 1870s until 1996. The nation's prime minister apologized, acknowledging the "incredibly harmful" policies, and pledged Can$321 million to support survivors.

While Canada is internationally associated with its stunning and bountiful natural environment, it is a top emitter of greenhouse gases. A 2019 government report indicated that Canada was warming up twice as fast as anywhere else in the world, and nearly three times faster in the north. The tension between recognizing the need for environmental protection and the reality of economic reliance on its natural resources is increasingly palpable. In 2020 and 2021, blockades around the Fairy Creek watershed on South Vancouver Island to protect British Colombia's old-growth forests became one of the largest acts of civil disobedience in Canadian history.

While the country has long been recognized for its role in multilateral diplomacy and as a broker of peace and security, foreign aid, and environmental protection, Prime Minister Justin Trudeau has struggled to remain relevant, given the growing strains within the rules-based international world order. His government faced the renegotiation of the NAFTA agreement that regulates trade between Canada, the United States, and Mexico, as well as the rise of populism and protectionism, specifically in the form of ex-President Trump's "Buy American" campaign. The 2021 snap election gave Trudeau a third term, though with a minority government.

COVID-19

Because health care in Canada is under provincial/ territorial jurisdiction there has been some variation in Covid-related policies and recommendations across the country. For example, high numbers of infections and deaths in long-term care facilities in Ontario and Quebec led to provincial reviews of care policies and procedures.

However, throughout the pandemic cooperation and coordination between the federal, provincial, regional, and local authorities in Canada remained generally good: by March 2022, more than 80 percent of Canadians were fully vaccinated against the virus, attesting to a high level of trust in health services and a (relatively) uniform political will to prevent illness and save lives.

Unfortunately, Canada's relatively successful handling of the pandemic was overshadowed by the trucker's strike in 2022. Though 90 percent of Canadian truckers were vaccinated, a vocal minority demonstrated against a requirement that all drivers reentering Canada be vaccinated. Though the unions did not support the action, large commercial trucks blocked the streets of the capital, Ottawa, for weeks, and also effectively closed a border crossing to the US in Alberta and the major trading route between the cities of Windsor and Detroit.

Various polls across the country indicated that there was little support for the goals, and certainly not for the tactics used. Many feared that the convoy represented a deep threat to democracy, incited and funded by the extreme right—evidenced by the flaunting of US Confederate flags, swastikas, and calls for freedom from the government. The protests were eventually dismantled through court injunctions, police action, and the prime minister's first ever invocation of the Emergencies Act.

CLIMATE CHANGE

According to the Web site Environment Canada, 2021 was "...most destructive, the most expensive, and the deadliest year for weather in Canadian history."

- Across Canada, a February freeze broke more than 225 new daily records for low minimum temperatures.
- In June, a "heat dome" covered British Columbia for eleven days, smashing record high temperatures and causing a wildfire that burned a village to the ground.
- A drought that covered southern regions from British Columbia to the eastern Prairies and Northwestern Ontario was extraordinary for its geographical breadth, severity, and length.
- In mid-November, an "atmospheric river" dumped more than 7.87 inches (200 mm) of rain on parts of British Columbia within 48 hours, putting entire communities underwater and forcing more than 17,000 people to evacuate their homes.
- Tornadoes in the east killed people for the first time in decades and Hurricane Larry knocked out power to 60,000 customers in Newfoundland.

CHAPTER TWO

VALUES & ATTITUDES

Canadians are generally proud of their nationality, in part because of the positive values this identity reflects: probably the most widely recognized of these are peacefulness, environmental friendliness, modesty, and equality. The large number of travelers who put the Canadian flag on their luggage can be seen as wanting to be associated with these positive attributes. Nationally, Canadians see themselves as a welcoming, open, and tolerant society. However, some of the major events in 2021 and early 2022 described in Chapter 1 have given their sense of national pride a beating.

Given the multiethnic mix and the geographic spread of the population, it is difficult to generalize about "Canadian" values and attitudes. This chapter looks at some common trends that Canadians find important, as individuals and collectively.

REGIONAL IDENTITIES

An often-asked question is whether Canadians form a nation or are rather a collection of regions. Factors that reinforce provincially shared experiences and loyalties include historical developments and immigration patterns, the huge distances between provincial urban centers, and the technical rules affecting labor mobility, as well as the fact that education is provincially administered. Canadians tend to take their holidays either locally or abroad, rather than in another Canadian province. Here we look briefly at elements that influence regional values.

People in the Atlantic Provinces

Quaerite prime regnum dei
(Seek ye first the kingdom of God)
Motto of Newfoundland and Labrador

Parva sub ingenti
(The small under the protection of the great)
Motto of Prince Edward Island

Munit haec et altera vincit
(One defends and the other conquers)
Motto of Nova Scotia

Spem reduxit
(She restored hope)
Motto of New Brunswick

The population of the four Atlantic provinces of Newfoundland and Labrador, New Brunswick, Prince Edward Island, and Nova Scotia is small (only around 2.4 million people). The majority are of Scottish, Irish, and English descent, with a sizable minority of French descent (the Acadians with their unique French dialect), and Indigenous Canadians. Slightly more than half the population live in cities and towns, and traditional values are strong. In the last five years, an increase in immigration to the region has broken the long-term trend of outmigration. Especially during the Covid-19 pandemic, the region attracted young people in particular, fleeing high prices and urban sprawl elsewhere. There are excellent universities in the region and a growing diversification of the labor market from its traditional fishing and agricultural base.

The local culture is influenced by the sea and fertile land for jobs, food, and incredible shorelines popular with tourists. The strong sense of community cohesion gave rise to the regional stereotype of being insular: those not born in the region remained outsiders—"from away." However, comparative post-Covid-19 surveys indicated that Atlantic Canadians were particularly open to immigration and diversity. The many good universities attract young people creating open, welcoming, and vibrant cities. Atlantic Canadians also appear to be optimistic and positive in outlook: nearly 80 percent were thankful to be living in Canada during the pandemic.

A special note on Newfoundland and Labrador: they only joined the Canadian Confederation in 1949, and some in the province still wonder if this was a good thing. Their accents are unique in Canada. They see themselves, and are seen by others, as being different from other Canadians—a factor which may explain why Newfoundlanders are the butt of many ("Newfie") jokes. These are neither representative nor much appreciated by the locals.

People in Quebec

> *Je me souviens*
> (I remember)
> Motto of Quebec

As far as the people of this province are concerned, there is Quebec and then there is the ROC—the rest of Canada. With 8.6 million inhabitants, this is Canada's second-most populous province (nearly a quarter of the national total). At the last census, 78 percent were Francophone, 7.45 percent were English speakers, and 42.6 percent considered themselves bilingual: there are Quebecois who speak little or no English!

The province has an aggressive language policy, which supports the preservation of the French language. Roads and shop signs are in French, Francophone parents must send their children to French schools, and there is a French-language bias in the immigration policy. This is in reaction to a former fear of losing the language; even as late as the 1960s, Francophone employees in Anglophone companies were forbidden to speak in French, for instance. Since the "Quiet Revolution" there has been a revival of pride in the language and culture, as seen in the rich music, film, and art scenes in the province. Surrounded by English-speakers on the North American continent, the Quebecois fear that if they don't protect their language they will lose it.

The Quebecois, particularly in the service sector not directly geared to tourism, may grumble when dealing with visitors in English. Generally, once they realize that the person is a foreigner and not an Anglophone Canadian, service may improve. For non-French speakers it is probably safe to say that there is an added hurdle to jump before getting to know the locals. Once you've done it, however, people are open and friendly; they have a good sense of humor, and are proud.

Humor on Both Sides

Age-old Francophone joke: "How many aspirin do Anglos take when they have a headache?" "Four—one for each corner."

Age-old Anglophone joke: "Why do French Canadians carry a frog in their pocket?" "For spare parts."

Canadian politics has often inflamed emotions between Anglophone and Francophone Canadians. To Anglophones, the Quebecois have been portrayed as troublemakers, ungrateful complainers, and stubborn egotists, and even, on one memorable occasion, as a contagious disease. To the Quebecois, Anglophones in other provinces have been portrayed as arrogant, domineering, narrow-minded, and mean-spirited.

French influence on Quebecois culture can be seen in every aspect of life, such as in body language (they use their hands more than the Anglo-Saxons), in dress style (they're more fashion-conscious than in the ROC), and in culinary taste (they love food and can talk about it interminably). But their culture is also quite distinct from that of France. Markedly North American in their values and social structures, they are, for instance, far less hierarchical in matters of social class and work environment than the French in Europe, far more polite in their interactions with each other, and less loud and quarrelsome. One of the attractions of the province is precisely this mix of old Europe and North America, particularly in a city like Quebec, which is a tourist hot spot.

People in Ontario

Ontario is home to the country's capital, Ottawa, and its largest city, Toronto. The population of nearly 15 million is concentrated in the largest conurbation in Canada, which takes up most of the southern half of the province: 94 percent of all Ontarians live in

Southern Ontario on 15 percent of the province's land area, making it one of the most densely populated areas in the country.

Ut incepit fidelis sic permanet
(Loyal she began, thus she remains)
Motto of Ontario

Its economy has the largest proportion of service and manufacturing industries, such as the automobile industry. As far as Ontarians are concerned, Ontario simply is the center of Canada, a sentiment that often has other Canadians bristling with indignation. While to outsiders Ontario may appear to be the essence of "Canada," the province is also its most culturally diverse: more than a quarter of its residents were born in another country. Toronto is known as the world's most multicultural city, more than half its population having been born elsewhere. The Francophone population is its largest minority.

If there is an old boy network anywhere in Canada, then it will be in Ontario. The economy makes it a highly competitive, dynamic environment. Ontarians generally believe that their province has everything: good jobs in a wide variety of sectors, culture and entertainment, a beautiful natural environment, and quaint towns and villages where all these can be found. They have busy lives and are accustomed to dealing with foreign visitors, who will probably feel comfortable in the cosmopolitan milieu.

People in the Prairies

Gloriosus et liber (Glorious and free)
Motto of Manitoba

Multis e gentibus vires
(From many peoples comes our strength)
Motto of Saskatchewan

Fortis et liber (Strong and free)
Motto of Alberta

Almost five million people live in the three prairie provinces of Manitoba, Saskatchewan, and Alberta: small populations in a huge territory with economies dominated by the exploitation of their natural resources.

In Manitoba, at the center of Canada, more than 55 percent of its population lives in the capital, Winnipeg. It is exceptional in the efforts of the indigenous (First Nations and Métis) populations to preserve their own unique cultures and traditions. Its highly diverse population has stimulated a distinctive, vibrant art and music scene. It is the location of Canada's oldest English-language theater, the Royal Manitoba Theatre Company, and Le Cercle Moliere, the nation's oldest French-language theater.

Saskatchewan is the most rural of the three, with one third of its population living in rural areas and a quarter in small urban centers. It continues to be Canada's breadbasket, dominated by large grain and beef cattle farms (the average size of a Saskatchewan farm is more than double the average size in the rest of Canada). The region's farming history has created a strong sense of community support, where hard work is valued.

Alberta is highly urbanized: 81 percent of its population live in urban areas and the Calgary–Edmonton corridor is the most densely populated area in Canada. At the same time, it has six UNESCO-designated World Heritage Sites and much of Canada's most breathtaking nature, making it a major tourist hub. It is generally considered the most conservative province in its pro-business and low tax stance. There are various theories about why this should be, including the notion that the original cattle rangers and large farmers were sensitive to government meddling in their businesses, just as today the oil and gas industry prefers its independence. While the province is indeed known for both its cowboy culture (rodeos, hats, boots—the works) and the "rednecks" in the oil and gas industry, its strong and diverse economy and high quality of life (it has the highest per capita GDP in Canada and even of many US states) attracts Canadians from across the country.

People of British Columbia

Splendor sine occasu
(Splendor undiminished)
Motto of British Columbia

BC, as it is popularly known, has been stereotyped as the lefty, trendy, drug-liberal, gay-friendly center of the country, a bit like LA to Americans. However, when cannabis was legalized across the entire nation in 2018, the province's supposed tolerance became less of a feature. What remains to support the preconception is perhaps the existence of nudist beaches, and the fact that Vancouver is the third-largest film production location in North America. The population of around five million is concentrated (60 percent) in two cities: Victoria, the capital, and Vancouver, Canada's third-largest city.

British Columbia, and particularly Vancouver, is highly multicultural. One third of its population has Asian heritage: Vancouver has North America's second-largest Chinese community. Many arrived in the late nineteenth century to build the Canadian Pacific Railway, and stayed. The Indigenous population of BC is experiencing a cultural revival that is more visible than in many other provinces. Seventy percent of the population claim English as their native tongue, and only 1.2 percent claim French.

People of the North

Nunavut Sanginivut
(Our land is our strength)
Motto of Nunavut

This region contains the Yukon, the Northwest Territories (NWT), and Nunavut. Together they cover more than a third of Canada's territory, but account for only 93,000 people. More than half of the citizens of the NWT and Nunavut and a quarter of those in the Yukon are Indigenous peoples. Here, the native languages are officially recognized along with English and French. Around 31 percent claim a native language as their mother tongue, though English is spoken by most people in the region. Half of all northerners live in small urban centers. Life here is thus highly community oriented. While it is true to say that everyone knows pretty well everyone else, visitors are warmly welcomed to this remote and beautiful part of the country.

CANADA'S PRIME MINISTERS

Prime ministers have predominantly come from Ontario and Quebec, a fact that many people in the other provinces and territories feel skewers Canadian politics toward the interests of those two provinces.

Name	Years in Office	Place of Birth
Pierre Trudeau	1968–1979, 1980–84	Quebec
Joe Clark	1979–1980	Alberta
John Turner	1984	England
Brian Mulroney	1984–1993	Quebec
Kim Campbell	1993	British Columbia
Jean Chrétien	1993–2003	Quebec
Paul Martin	2003–2006	Ontario
Stephen Harper	2006–2015	Ontario
Justin Trudeau	2015–present	Quebec

BILINGUALISM

As we've seen, Canadians are, for the most part, not French–English bilingual. The *country* is "bilingual," in that it has two official languages and federal services need to be provided in both languages. But nationwide, only around 18 percent of the population claim to be bilingual in French and English. Quebec is predominantly Francophone, where a majority of the population speaks primarily French; the rest of Canadians are primarily Anglophone, and speak no French.

How people value bilingualism depends on where they live; the closer one is to Ontario and Quebec, the greater the acceptance of bilingualism as a value and a skill. In Quebec, since the 1970s, successive governments have encouraged the use of the French language. Recently, however, the Quebecois have come to realize that mastering the English language is an asset in today's global economy.

The largest French communities outside Quebec are in the Atlantic Provinces and Ontario; these provinces are generally more supportive of bilingualism than elsewhere. The further west you go, however, the less obvious the advantage of French–English bilingualism becomes.

MULTICULTURALISM

Canada takes in 1 percent of its population annually, which means that approximately one in five Canadians

People gathering to watch the Canada Day parade in downtown Montreal.

is born outside the country. One reason immigration is not the hot issue it is elsewhere in the world is Canada's "smart selection" policy, whereby immigrants are admitted according to skills-based criteria. With an aging population it is clear to most people that immigration is necessary to maintain social services and economic growth. However, Canada is in the throes of a unique experiment that affects the values and attitudes of all Canadians. As one of the world's leading immigration nations, it fosters the value of tolerance like no other nation today.

Finding ways of ensuring that cultural groups not only cohabit peacefully but actively create a society together is vital, given that there are more than two hundred ethnic groups in Canada; around 30 percent of the population are immigrants to the country, and nearly 18 percent are Canadian children born to immigrant parents or "new arrivals" (meaning that they were not born in Canada); nearly one in five schoolchildren in Vancouver and Toronto are new arrivals; and around 13 percent of the population are "visible minorities" (meaning that they are "persons, other than Aboriginal people, who are non-Caucasian in race or non-white in color").

In 1988, the Canadian government passed the Official Multiculturalism Act, which established the equal rights of all Canadians, regardless of their culture of origin, religion, gender, and so on. They soon realized that this "live and let live" approach was not enough to ensure the creation of a tolerant society free of racism. Toward the end of the 1990s, the government added an antiracism approach to its multicultural policy. The goal of these policies is to create a society where there is equality not only in the opportunities people have but also in the actual outcomes of how they live and work.

Canadians differentiate their multicultural, immigrant society from the American version of the "melting pot" with the idea of a "cultural mosaic." The melting pot idea is associated with assimilation (meaning that people give up their original culture in order to become part of the new society) creating a unified "American" society. The theory behind the Canadian multicultural mosaic is that immigrants are not pressed to give up their culture and are free to find a balance between old and new. This means that ideally cultural groups live alongside one another in tolerant coexistence.

TOLERANCE

Though few Canadians would argue against the country's immigration policy, it cannot be said that there is no racism in Canada, or resistance to change.

In the past, Canada attempted to force indigenous peoples to assimilate into mainstream "Canadian" culture, and they continue to experience discrimination and negative stereotyping. The discovery of unmarked graves of indigenous children in residential schools forced the nation to recognize not only the brutality of the system but also to face up to the national "blind eye" to the plight of Canada's indigenous peoples generally.

Also, immigrants, even Americans and Western Europeans, may face difficulties when looking for jobs. Immigrants are selected on a points system, based on the skills and knowledge required for the Canadian labor pool. However, when they arrive they are faced with residency, license, or certification requirements that mean many cannot work in their professions without costly and time-consuming retraining or exams. Many immigrants feel discriminated against for not being "local" or for not having work experience in that province.

The social and economic difficulties faced by new immigrants, especially those from developing countries who are visible or linguistic minorities, is recognized as a problem in Canada. The issue is primarily urban and is being addressed through programs such as support for heritage language training, sensitization of school boards to pluralism, and aid to ethnic social services.

Visitors, however, will most probably find that the Canadians they meet are tolerant of differences. Visitors may even find Canadians tolerant to the point of appearing uninterested. The fact that a stranger comes from another country is not unique or novel to a Canadian, and they may not think to inquire about a visitor's home country. Also, while the media in Canada does cover international news (much more than it does in the USA), "the rest of the world" still appears very far away to your average Canadian.

RELIGION

In Canada, religious conviction is considered to be purely personal in nature. There is a de facto separation between the powers of the Church and state, and the freedom to practice the faith of one's choice is a constitutionally protected right. The number of Canadians with no attachment to an organized religion is growing rapidly.

Just over sixty-three percent of Canadians claim to be Christian. Over half of these are Catholic. Fewer than 10 percent are of a non-Christian faith. Nearly one quarter of Canadians claim to have no religious affiliation. Wiccans and other neo-pagans, and Native Canadian Spirituality, are the fastest growing non-Christian faiths. Representation of other non-Christian beliefs, such as Islam and several Eastern religions, is growing due primarily to immigration.

DON'T SAY "AMERICAN"

"Canadians are generally indistinguishable from the Americans, and the surest way of telling the two apart is to make the observation to a Canadian."

American journalist Richard Starnes

Part of the difficulty in generalizing about Canadian values and attitudes is the fact that identity is often expressed in negative terms. In English Canada this boils down to "We are not the same as Americans" and in Quebec this equates to "We are neither French nor Anglophone."

In the English-speaking provinces, this has practically become a cliché, but it is just about the only generalization that everyone will agree on: Canadians are not Americans. In fact, Canadians spend quite a lot of time and energy underlining the differences between themselves and Americans. There is a slight "inferiority complex" on the part of Canadians that may explain why, if you unwittingly ask a Canadian abroad if they are American, you are likely to get an

Supporter of the Freedom Convoy demonstrating against the vaccine mandate.

indignant answer. It's nothing personal, just a reflection of a geopolitical sensitivity.

The truckers' strike of early 2022 highlighted how Canadian values differ. One fundamental ideology of the "Freedom Convoy" was the defense of individual rights: the freedom of an individual not to wear a mask or be vaccinated. However, the majority of Canadians accept that the rights of the individual should be balanced against the possibility that they could endanger the health or freedom of others.

In terms of their behavior, Canadians see themselves as less arrogant and loud than their southern neighbors. One can display character and defend one's own, or someone else's, rights, but modesty and respect must be maintained. The national equalization and health care programs are popular in the country, indicating

the importance of community values: Canadians
see themselves as being less individualistic than
Americans.

In fact, visitors to Canada may be surprised
by the amount of America-bashing that goes on
there. In Canada, it is not "done" to criticize other
cultures—except that of America. Putting down their
superpower neighbor, which Canadians feel at once
intimidated by and superior to, is a national pastime.

> "Living next to the United States is in some way
> like sleeping with an elephant. No matter how
> friendly and even tempered the beast, one is
> affected by every twitch and grunt."
> Former prime minister Pierre Elliott Trudeau

NICE PEOPLE

> "Canadians are an ambivalent lot:
> One minute they're peacekeepers,
> next minute they punch the hell out of
> each other on the ice rink."
> Journalist Ken Wiwa

Though they may have difficulty defining their
culture, Canadians are mostly "very proud" of being
Canadian. However, they are not overtly nationalistic
and will not scream this love from the rooftops.
To explain this muted patriotism, Canadians, both

Francophone and Anglophone, will tell you that it is because they value modesty. This accent on humility also explains why so few famous Canadians and well-known Canadian inventions are recognized as being Canadian. However, there is another explanation for their lack of patriotism: Canadians reserve the right to grumble. They love to complain, particularly about their government: talking about the weather and griping about the government are two major topics of conversation at almost any gathering.

An international stereotype of Canadians is that they are soft-spoken, unassuming, and peace-loving. Just think of the country's multilateral role in peacekeeping and other UN contexts. Canadian backpackers and tourists are generally welcomed as respectful, interested, and unobtrusive guests. (So much so that Americans have been known to travel with Canadian flags on their luggage or a red maple leaf on their lapel.)

Canadians are polite, almost to a fault. This is why, if you step on someone's foot, they say "sorry" (for having put their foot in the wrong place). They are very careful not to offend anyone. This is one reason Canadians are so careful about not asking direct questions—lest they seem impolite or nosy, or just plain stupid. It is noticeable that crowds are respectful of other people's space needs; Canadians have large "personal space bubbles," which may have something to do with the generous amount of physical space they have to share. Shopkeepers are pleasant and helpful, without being overly friendly or aggressively present.

ATTITUDES TOWARD WOMEN

For women, traveling in Canada is a generally pleasant experience. It would be going too far to say that men and women are equal in Canadian society: as in many other countries, women often bear the brunt of the burden of child-rearing even when they work as hard as their husbands, and pay is not always equal. It is estimated that women working full-time across all sectors earn on average 71 percent of what men do. Women hold 25 percent of seats in the Lower House, and make up 31 percent of the cabinet; Canada was the eighth-best country on the UNDP's Gender Inequality Index.

However, women were given the right to vote in 1918, and in 2013 women represented 47.3 percent of the labor force. It would be very bad form to assume that the woman in the office is the secretary—she may be the boss.

INDIVIDUALISTIC COLLECTIVISTS

Canadian society is North American in that it is cosmopolitan (urban and multicultural) and middle class. Europeans who immigrate to Canada speak with sighs of relief about the apparent looser system of social controls. There is a lack of class consciousness, something that Canadians are quite proud of. This does not mean that it is a classless society, but that status is related to financial wealth and not birthright, accent, or old school tie. There is no aristocracy, or barrier to jobs because of the school you attended, though, like anywhere, who you know and what you look like probably still counts.

Canadian society is structured on a capitalistic economic system based on meritocracy, which values hard work and individual responsibility. However, it is also based on a generous welfare system that aims to equalize the standard of living of its citizens. Higher taxes set limits to wealth accumulation, and wage controls mean that some individuals would earn far more if they worked in the USA. American surgeons, for instance, earn three times more than their Canadian counterparts. Canadians are generally proud and fiercely defensive of their system of universal health care (it is simply a nonnegotiable part of being a citizen).

Thus, while on the one hand Canadians value the rights of individuals to their own beliefs, religion, and so on, they are collectivist in that they are willing to accept limits to personal freedoms in support of collective values such as peace, justice, respect for authority, and equality under the welfare system.

GOOD CITIZENS

Canadians consider themselves to be law-abiding citizens. This belief may come from a comparison with the United States, where violent crime statistics are much higher: most types of crime have been decreasing and are at their lowest since 1972.

Where does this peaceful image come from? One contributory factor is that the majority of Canadians are respectful of authority. There is a belief that rules are there for a good reason: the government is there to take care of its citizens, and its rules should therefore be kept. While around seven million Canadians own guns (primarily for recreational hunting), city-dwellers tend to disapprove of guns, and a long list of assault weapons are banned. In the past few decades, high-profile murders, "acts of terrorism," and corruption cases have shown that Canada is neither crime-proof nor immune to international developments.

Also, a great deal of attention is paid to prevention. Prevention strategies seep through every aspect of Canadian life. The entire health service system is focused on the prevention of sickness and the spread of disease; traffic is ultra-regulated in order to minimize accidents; breads or candies are individually wrapped so that if someone puts their hand in the jar others will not catch any infection (or be deliberately poisoned . . .).

ENVIRONMENTALLY FRIENDLY?

Canadians care about their environment, as attested by the enthusiastic use of the thousands of national and provincial parks, reserves, wilderness, and recreational areas for sports and leisure activities. Survey after survey indicate that a majority of Canadians worry about climate change and believe that an energy transition is inevitable. The deadly heat domes, destructive wildfires, and historic flooding of 2021 were seen as clear signs of the impact of Canada's rapidly warming climate.

However, the same surveys indicate that people's willingness to fund change and adjust their lifestyles is limited. While this is not unique to Canada, the tension between pro-environment sentiment and economic goals is. A significant portion of the national GDP comes from extractive industries such as mining, forestry, and oil and gas. Extracting and processing crude from Canada's oil sands (the largest deposit of crude on the planet) creates up to three times more greenhouse gas emissions than traditional extraction techniques; it requires the stripping of forests and wetlands, and produces quantities of toxic waste. Balancing the tension between a deep love of Canada's natural environment and the economic exploitation of that same environment is a challenge: the anti-logging protest on Vancouver Island in 2021–22 was the largest in the country's history. It likely won't be the last.

DON'T ROCK THAT BOAT!

A classic Canadian stereotype is that they are "don't rock the boat" types who prefer moderation and feel most comfortable within the status quo. All stereotypes begin with a grain of truth: Canada is largely middle class; its people tend toward the political center, and are culturally mindful about keeping their opinions to themselves lest they be mistaken for their "loud" and "brash" neighbors to the south.

However, political discourse can get nasty, as was seen during the trucker's "Freedom Convoy" in 2022. Corruption and the extreme right are present. And so is the increasing influence of "wokeness" from the "extreme" left. An example is the nationwide debate about freedom of speech in Canada's universities and how woke culture is stifling free and open discussion in the name of equity and antiracism. As with the "radical right" anti-vax discourse, the language and woke standpoint are thought by many to originate in, and be more representative of issues in, the United States.

It is unclear how Canadian culture will be affected by the impact of a more radical discourse on both the left and the right. The cultural tendency of wanting to be polite and not hurt people's feelings has perhaps been harnessed by "woke culture" and influenced the debates, particularly in schools and on university campuses. It is safe to say that Canadians are not renowned for being avant-garde or for risk-taking behavior.

CHAPTER THREE

CUSTOMS & TRADITIONS

We have seen that Canada as a nation is not only relatively new; it is also composed of a very broad variety of ethnic groups. Each has its religious and cultural customs: weddings, birthdays, and all other such "life events" are defined by community ties, historical influences, and modern expressions of these.

NATIONAL HOLIDAYS AND CELEBRATIONS

There are three types of holiday in Canada: statutory holidays, civic holidays, and events that are celebrated but are not free days. For statutory holidays, employers are obliged to offer their staff a day off work or pay a supplementary salary. Each province and territory is free to determine how many statutory holidays employees are entitled to. This varies from six to eight a year in most areas, with the notable exception of Newfoundland and Labrador, where there are fourteen. On these days, most offices will close, as will government services, schools, and banks. Public services, such as public transportation, will work to a reduced schedule.

Civic holidays are celebrations that are recognized as an important day in the calendar, but employers can decide on an individual basis whether or not to give their employees a paid day off. There are federal and provincial holidays of both types.

Finally, there are celebrations that are not holidays in the sense of time off work or school, but which are celebrated after hours. Valentine's Day, Mother's and Father's Day, and Halloween are examples of such events.

Canada Day

This statutory holiday is celebrated on July 1. In the major cities across the country it is celebrated with fireworks, parades, and open-air concerts—a great street party that brings out the crowds. But even this most important of days is less uniformly celebrated than one might expect.

In two provinces Canada Day takes a slightly different turn. In Quebec, the first day of July is the first day of all rental agreements for apartments everywhere in the province. Therefore Canada Day is jokingly called Moving Day. It is celebrated with concerts and events, but is more subdued than in the rest of the country since the event is outcompeted by Quebec's "National Day." (See page 91.)

Canada Day parade on Georgia Street, Vancouver.

In Newfoundland and Labrador, Canada Day is known as Memorial Day and is observed on the Monday nearest July 1. On this day the province commemorates its heavy losses during the First World War in the Battle of Beaumont-Hamel, on the first day of the Battle of the Somme in 1916.

Labour Day

Labour Day (spelled with a "u," in Canada) is celebrated on the first Monday in September, the same day as in the United States (not May 1, as in many other countries). While few Canadians and no Americans know it, the North American Labor Day celebrations started in Canada with the organization of several parades in 1872 in Toronto and Ottawa. These were demonstrations aimed at freeing twenty-four imprisoned leaders of the typographical union, who had gone on strike to obtain a nine-hour working day. After the success of these events, which saw the legalization of unions, traditional parades and picnics became a yearly event in Canada. The first such parade in the USA was held on September 5, 1882, after the visit of a leading American trade unionist to an event in Toronto. In 1894, the Canadian Parliament declared a national holiday for Labour Day.

For most Canadians today, however, this is the last long weekend of the summer, as schools always start on the following Tuesday. Many people go on short vacations or go shopping for fall and winter clothing and school supplies. If you are in Canada on business, don't plan to get much accomplished during this weekend.

Thanksgiving

This is not the same celebration as in the United States and is not held on the same day. In Canada, Thanksgiving falls on the second Monday in October, and its origins are different. Historically, thanksgiving days were proclaimed for a variety of reasons: in 1814, for example, it was to give thanks for the "end of sanguinary contest in Europe and to give the Dominions blessings of peace." In 1833 it gave thanks for the cessation of cholera. The first Thanksgiving Day in the Dominion of Canada was on April 15, 1872, to celebrate the recovery of the Prince of Wales (later King Edward VII) from a serious illness. Only in 1879 was its stated purpose to give thanks for "the blessings of an abundant harvest"—what it is traditionally thought to be. It has thus little to do with the survival of the original colonists in the harsh conditions of the New World. Today, it is celebrated modestly, if at all, with a family meal.

KEY HOLIDAYS AND CELEBRATIONS

New Year's Day	January 1	Statutory
Family Day	Third Monday in February	Varies by province
Good Friday	Date varies	Statutory
Easter Monday	Date varies	Statutory
Commonwealth Day	First Monday in March	Civic
Victoria Day	Monday preceding May 25	Statutory
National Indigenous People's Day	June 21	Civic
Canadian Multiculturalism Day	June 27	Civic
Canada Day	July 1	Statutory
Civic Holiday	First Monday in August	Civic or statutory by province or territory
Labour Day	First Monday in September	Statutory
Thanksgiving Day	Second Monday in October	Statutory
Remembrance Day	November 11	Civic
Christmas Day	December 25	Statutory
Boxing Day	December 26	Statutory

Victoria Day

This statutory holiday is celebrated on the last Monday in May, originally to commemorate Queen Victoria's birthday. Today it honors the current sovereign, King

Charles III. Across Canada this long weekend is seen as the unofficial start of the summer, when attractions open for the first time, or when people open up their cottages or summerhouses after the long winter. If the weather is fine, it is a lovely day to be in the countryside.

Predictably, this holiday has an entirely different raison d'être in Quebec. Since 2003 the day has been called National Patriots' Day, to honor the rebellion against the British in 1837. This is, of course, the antithesis of the point of Victoria Day—but you can do that in Canada.

Remembrance Day

Observed on November 11, Remembrance Day is a statutory holiday throughout all of Canada except Ontario and Quebec. The celebrations on this day commemorate the Canadians who died in the First and Second World Wars and the Korean War, as well as all the peacekeeping operations in which Canada has been involved.

Artificial poppies are sold by the Royal Canadian Legion to raise money for needy veterans and are very popular on this day. While poppies are a symbol of remembrance in many countries, the tradition of wearing an artificial poppy on Remembrance Day has a specific history in Canada.

Veterans at a Remembrance Day ceremony in Abbotsford, British Columbia.

This tradition stems from the poem "In Flanders Fields," written in 1915 by Lieutenant-Colonel John McCrae, who was a Canadian Medical Officer during the First World War.

IN FLANDERS FIELDS

In Flanders fields the poppies blow
Between the crosses, row on row,
That mark our place; and in the sky
The larks, still bravely singing, fly
Scarce heard amid the guns below.

We are the Dead. Short days ago
We lived, felt dawn, saw sunset glow,
Loved, and were loved, and now we lie
In Flanders fields.

Take up our quarrel with the foe:
To you from failing hands we throw
The torch; be yours to hold it high.
If ye break faith with us who die
We shall not sleep, though poppies grow
In Flanders fields.

Christmas

A national event launched in 1986 is the annual "Christmas Lights across Canada." Public parks and buildings are decorated with colored lights, and the switch is turned on at exactly 6:45 p.m. in each time zone on the first Thursday in December, creating a wave of light from east to west and theoretically uniting Canadians across all the time zones.

How families celebrate Christmas varies between provinces, ethnic groups, and families. For instance, in Quebec, families traditionally go to midnight mass and return home to a feast and the visit of Santa Claus to the house. Under the Christmas tree, the crèche (a model nativity village) is spread out around the crib.

In Newfoundland and Labrador there is a tradition during Christmas week for people to "fish for the church." They bring their catch of fish to be sold for the local parish church. During the Christmas Eve service, children hold little lighted candles in a turnip saved from the harvest for this purpose. Mummering, in which people disguise themselves and go visiting from house to house, is practiced here but is little known elsewhere in Canada.

Christmas trees in public places have been the target of multicultural debates in recent years. In Christian homes the trees are decorated with strings of colored lights and bright baubles. Large family meals of special foods such as ham or turkey are served, and of course the tradition of unwrapping the gifts brought by Santa Claus and left under the tree or in a stocking hung from the mantelpiece is a major family event.

Boxing Day, December 26, is spent recovering from the excesses of the Christmas celebrations and is particularly known in Canada as a day of great post-Christmas sales.

Commonwealth Day

The idea of celebrating Commonwealth Day—the Commonwealth is a voluntary association of fifty-six countries most of which were formerly British colonies—came from the former Canadian prime minister Pierre Elliott Trudeau in 1977. He wanted to set aside one day each year on which all Commonwealth countries could mark their membership, renew their commitment to the association, and encourage an understanding of its aims. It is celebrated on the second Monday of March, and Canadians notice its arrival primarily through schoolchildren, for whom special activities are organized. Commonwealth countries represent a quarter of all humanity, and the yearly themes are intended to support the creation of a harmonious global environment.

Earth Day

Celebrated every April 22, Earth Day is the largest, most celebrated environmental event worldwide. It is worth mentioning here because nearly every schoolchild in Canada takes part in an Earth Day activity, such as planting a tree.

Family Day

The provinces of Alberta, British Columbia, New Brunswick, Ontario, and Saskatchewan celebrate Family Day as a civic holiday. In Manitoba, this date is known as Louis Riel Day in honor of the Métis leader of the Red River Resistance of 1869–70, who was instrumental in drafting the List of Rights that formed the basis of the Manitoba Act. He was instrumental in Manitoba becoming Canada's fifth province according to his vision of a province that embraces all its cultures. In Nova Scotia this date is celebrated as Heritage Day, and as Islander Day in Prince Edward Island.

Flag Day

This celebration shows just how new some of Canada's traditions are. On February 15, 1996, the prime minister, Jean Chrétien, proclaimed that every February 15 would be known as Flag Day, to commemorate the first time the maple leaf flag was raised over Parliament Hill, in 1965.

PROVINCIAL HOLIDAYS

Each province and territory also has its own statutory or civic holidays, reflecting the nature of its specific history and cultural influences. Many have a heritage day or provincial day on the first Monday in August in which cultural activities are organized.

The **Alberta Family Day** is a civic holiday (so not everyone gets the day off) that is celebrated every third Monday in February. The holiday was proclaimed by the premier of the time, Don Getty, in 1990 when his son, Dale, was arrested for possession of cocaine and was revealed to be addicted. Premier Getty admitted publicly that he had neglected his family and stressed

PROCLAMATION OF NATIONAL FLAG OF CANADA DAY

"At the stroke of noon on February 15, 1965, Canada's red and white maple leaf flag was raised for the very first time.

The flag belongs to all Canadians; it is an emblem we all share.

Although simple in design, Canada's flag well reflects the common values we hold so dear: freedom, peace, respect, justice, and tolerance. Canada's flag is a symbol that unites Canadians and expresses throughout the world and always our pride in being Canadian.

The maple leaf flag pays homage to our geography, reflects the grandeur of our history and represents our national identity.

Our flag thus honours Canadians of all origins who, through their courage and determination, have helped to build and are continuing to build our great country: a dynamic country that is open to the future.

Therefore, I, Jean Chrétien, Prime Minister of Canada, declare that February 15 will be celebrated henceforth as National Flag of Canada Day.

Let us be proud of our flag! Let us recognize how privileged we are to live in Canada, this magnificent country that encompasses our history, our hopes, our future."

Jean Chrétien, twentieth prime minister of Canada

the importance for all Albertans to spend time with their families.

There are several holidays that are recognized only in Newfoundland and Labrador. They celebrate **St. Patrick's Day** (the patron saint of Ireland) on the nearest Monday to March 17. Also, in a tribute to their Protestant Irish roots, many communities in Newfoundland and Labrador hold **Orangemen's Day** celebrations on July 12, which commemorate the Protestant victory over the Roman Catholic forces of the deposed James II in the Battle of the Boyne in 1690 in Ireland. In tribute to their English roots, many also celebrate **St. George's Day** (the patron saint of England) on the nearest Monday to April 23. **Discovery Day** is celebrated on the Monday nearest June 24 in commemoration of the discovery of the province in 1497 by John Cabot. Since 1997, it has also been known as **Cabot 500 Day**.

Although **National Indigenous Peoples Day** is a nationally recognized day on June 21 (the summer solstice), it is a statutory holiday only in the Northwest Territories. This celebration was established in 1996 because ". . . the Aboriginal peoples of Canada have made and continue to make valuable contributions to Canadian society and it is considered appropriate that there be, in each year, a day to mark and celebrate these contributions and to recognize the different cultures of the Aboriginal people of Canada."

Quebec province has a few idiosyncratic celebrations that relate to its history and cultural heritage. **St. Jean**

Pow Wow dancers in Ottawa on National Indigenous Peoples Day.

Baptist, or National Day, or St. John's Day (la Saint-Jean), as it is also known, has been a legal holiday in Quebec since 1925. Celebrated on June 24, it honors the patron saint of Quebec, John the Baptist, though today its multiple cultural festivals highlight the talents of Quebec's musicians and artists. In terms of the size and scope of the events on the day, it rivals the efforts of the federal government's Canada Day festivities.

Another anomaly in Quebec is the **Construction Holiday**, which takes place during the last two weeks of July. Though it applies officially only to the construction industry, many other Quebecois take their vacations during these two weeks. Visitors to Quebec would do well to take note of these dates; it is a great time to be on holiday in the province but not propitious for the ambitious business visitor.

In the Yukon Territory, **Klondike Gold Discovery Day** is a public holiday celebrated on the Friday before August 17. It commemorates the anniversary of the discovery of gold in 1896. This event started the Klondike Gold Rush, which was one of the largest gold rushes in North America. At its peak, Dawson City had a population of 40,000. Once the gold rush was over, the city dwindled to its current population of under 2,000, a town that attracts around 60,000 tourists a year.

OTHER TRADITIONS

Hockey Night in Canada

One of the few weekly rituals that is observed nationwide is watching Hockey Night in Canada (HNIC). This is the television broadcast every Saturday night of the National Hockey League (NHL) games, which embrace teams from both the US and Canada. This tradition started in 1959 (on the radio it started in 1933) making it the world's oldest sports program on television. While Canadian teams are not doing as well in the NHL as they used to, the program is still one of the most highly rated Canadian programs on TV. The theme song to the program is known as Canada's second national anthem. The real national anthem is sung at the beginning of each game, half in French and half in English. This bilingual version is more familiar to many Canadians than either single-language version.

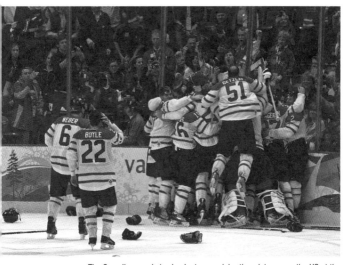

The Canadian men's ice hocky team celebrating victory over the US at the Vancouver Winter Olympics.

A Modern National Hero

Terry Fox was born in 1958 in British Columbia. He lost his right leg to cancer at the age of nineteen. In April 1980 he set out on his Marathon of Hope, in which he intended to run across Canada in order to raise money for cancer research. He died in 1981 of lung cancer after completing 3,331 miles (5,373 km). He was an inspiration across the world, and today the Terry Fox Run is held annually in Canada and in sixty other countries. More than a million people take part, and it is the largest single fund-raising event for cancer research in the world.

Graduation Rings

A rather more solemn tradition is the "Ritual of Calling the Engineer," also known as the Iron Ring ceremony. This ceremony is officially copyrighted in Canada and is thus unique to the country.

In 1922 the seven past presidents of the Engineering Institute of Canada met in Montreal. One of them, H. E. T. Haultain, Professor of Civil Engineering at the University of Toronto, felt that something was needed to bind the profession of Canadian engineers. He wrote to Rudyard Kipling, several of whose poems had featured engineers, and asked him to devise an oath and ceremony that would serve as a statement of ethics for engineers across the country. Kipling responded with enthusiasm, and in 1923 provided the "Camp of Seven Wardens" with the "Ritual of Calling the Engineer." Precise details of the ceremonies vary from university to university, but they are always based on Kipling's original vision.

The ceremony also includes the giving of the Iron Ring (a version of a school ring). There is a myth surrounding the Iron Ring that heightens the pledge made by engineers during the ceremony. The story is that the first rings were made from the wreckage of the Quebec Bridge, which collapsed during construction in 1907 because of an error in the design engineer's calculations. The bridge was redesigned, but collapsed again in 1916 when its center span fell while being hoisted into place. The bridge was finally completed in 1917.

The first Ritual of Calling the Engineer ceremony was held at the University of Toronto in 1925. It is a voluntary ceremony and does not confer the right to work as an engineer; a degree is given at a separate graduation ceremony. This event reminds engineers of their moral and societal obligations, the goal of adhering solemnly to the highest ideals, to humbly serve society with the knowledge and skills they have gained.

Festivals

Long, warm summer days sees cultural festivals sprout across the country, showcasing local heritage, traditions, cultures, and the arts. Vancouver's **Dragon Boat Festival**

Racing in Toronto's International Dragon Boat Festival.

Bagpipers marching in the Calgary Stampede Parade, Alberta.

in June, the **Calgary Stampede** in July, and the **Acadian Festival** in New Brunswick in August, are among the largest and best known. Even in the coldest periods of winter many cities host events like Quebec

Snowtubing on the Plains of Abraham during Quebec City's Winter Carnival.

City's **Winter Carnival**, and **Winterlude** in the country's capital, Ottawa. For the more adventurous, Saskatchewan hosts the **Canadian Challenge Sled Dog Race** at the end of February on the same 320-mile track used historically by First Nations people and fur trappers.

Yard Sales

If you happen to be driving around on summer weekends, you may come across a "yard sale" or two. These are common across Canada. It is legal to set up a sign in your front garden, put your old stuff out on the driveway, prepare a jug of lemonade or iced tea, and wait for visitors. Some sales are small, family-run events, some are organized by a group of neighbors, and others are arranged through a community center or other local organization.

Berry Picking

Another popular weekend activity is berry picking. Berries and other fruits become ripe for picking throughout the summer and early fall, starting with strawberries and ending with cherries, apples, and peaches. Some fruits grow wild, such as blueberries or raspberries in the Lac Saint Jean area of Quebec, but people often go to local farms to pick whatever is in season. You pay for the amount you pick, which you then take home and make into pies and jams—or just eat fresh with cream.

CHAPTER FOUR

MAKING FRIENDS

FRIENDSHIP

Canadians dedicate much of their free time to family. As for friends, they have different circles, from the close inner ties of family and "best" friends through to those whom they see once a year for a reunion. Canadians are not cliquey; a friendship begins when people enjoy being together—full stop. A friendship can be a deep, long-term relationship or more superficial, based on a common interest—a particular sport, for example—or simple enjoyment of one another's company. Canadians make friends throughout their school careers, in all their clubs and activities, at work, in their place of worship, and among neighbors. Social circles are flexible since friendship circles change over a lifetime.

This is good news for visitors, because it means that Canadians are generally open to meeting new people and making new friends.

In order to meet Canadians in any significant way, a visitor will need to share a common interest that brings them into repeated contact. One could even start up a jolly evening of discussions in a bar if conditions were right. Contact can be made through work, through a sport, or through an intellectual or artistic activity such as a book club or painting group. However, even business visitors to Canada note how friendly and easy Canadians are to get to know. One doesn't have to be a good friend to be invited to someone's home for dinner or drinks—though this happens comparatively rarely. It is more usual to be invited to an after-work drink with your coworker's team on Fridays. On weekends, cottage owners may extend an invitation to a close friend or colleague to spend a day or two with them, or rent a cottage together with friends for holidays or a short summer break. Friends often spend time in the outdoors, enjoying sports such as mountain biking, trekking, canoeing on the many lakes, white-water rafting, paddle-boarding, and playing beach volleyball in summer, or skating, skiing, and snowboarding in winter. Younger, single friends like to travel abroad in groups and book activities together such as yoga retreats, vacationing on the beach, and scuba diving and sailing.

INVITATIONS HOME

Canadians do entertain at home. If you are invited, it will probably be an informal occasion, such as drinks or

Group of friends at a restaurant in the ski resort of Whistler, British Columbia.

a casual meal with the family. It is customary to bring a small something for the host or hostess, such as a bottle of wine, flowers, or a plant. Unless people know each other very well, they never just pop in unannounced. Even family members call beforehand.

When you arrive, you will be expected to take off your shoes in most homes. In winter, people wear boots or rubber overshoes outside in the mushy snow and on icy sidewalks. These are hot, dirty, and hardly fashionable, so for offices and homes people carry indoor shoes with them in a plastic bag. Especially in someone's home, you should take your boots off so as not to tread snow and salt into the living room rug. In case the idea of spending an evening barefoot or in your socks makes you uncomfortable, it is not seen as unusual, even in the summer, if you bring a pair of indoor shoes with you. Unlike in some Asian countries, Canadians do not provide slippers for you to use.

One more little thing: if you need to use the lavatory, ask for the "washroom" or "bathroom." The word "toilet" is not a polite term in Canada, though everyone will understand where you want to go.

GOOD MANNERS

Canadians are polite through and through. It goes further than just "please" and "thank you," which you should say at every conceivable opportunity: "Would you pass the sugar, please?" must be followed by "Thank you," which will be followed by "You're welcome." Canadians are aware of the impact of what they say on other people; small children are taught about their own space bubble and how to respect each other's spatial needs. Many Canadians, though not all, would never dream of complaining about bad service in a restaurant. They would prefer to avoid a conflict— rather than make a fuss they will not tip the waiter and simply never return.

This means that if something irritates you during your visit, the chances are that it won't be rude or aggressive behavior; and also, if you make a social blunder, you may never find out because no one will mention it! This point shouldn't be taken too seriously: there are people of many nationalities in Canada, who all do things differently. However, the ground rule is that they do appreciate it when people are courteous and mild-mannered. If you notice that people's feathers are ruffled, just apologize, and all will be forgiven. But for your own peace of mind, follow a few tips on treading softly with Canadians.

Some visitors to Canada remark on how open Canadians are to talking about all sorts of deep or personal topics. There are taboos (see overleaf), but Canadians are willing to take on many difficult topics and discuss them, or share their opinions. When asking a direct question, a Canadian will be careful to avoid putting the other person in the position of having to answer. When asked a direct question, a Canadian will most probably answer honestly, or as honestly as possible. Thus asking direct questions, particularly about personal issues, can be touchy. But if someone starts on a topic, then be prepared for a good conversation. For example, a Canadian probably wouldn't ask such a question as, "When are you going to get another boyfriend?" but if information is offered, the door to the conversation is opened, and that's all that is required.

If you want to make a point in a discussion with Canadians, don't use the "hard sell" approach. They appreciate a good listener, a modest presentation of ideas, and a bit of humor where possible. They enjoy a debate, but bear in mind that you are all sharing opinions, so it's all right to agree to disagree. French Canadians are more emotional, and use far more body language and expression. They are, however, just as polite as the Anglophones in other parts of the country. In recent years, "woke" culture from across the southern border has been embraced by some, and this makes it riskier to start a conversation on certain subjects that could cause offense or turn out to be sensitive for the people present. It is therefore advisable to let your hosts pick the topics of conversation, and not to demonstrate a strong stance on anything in particular.

In general, shaking hands with both men and women is common in formal settings such as an office. English-speaking Canadians tend to be less tactile than Francophones; Anglophone friends, for instance, may just say "Hello" to each other in informal situations. French Canadian men (colleagues, friends, and acquaintances) will always shake hands. In informal situations between friends, men and women, and two women, will kiss twice on the cheeks. Family members may kiss on the lips—aunts to adult nieces and nephews, for instance. But for newcomers, a nice firm handshake will do.

TABOOS

Criticizing Canada and highlighting the similarities between Canadians and Americans are conversation stoppers. Another way to displease your hosts is to point out how Canada's Native Peoples have not been treated equally, despite the country's dedication to multicultural principles. Also, questioning the quality and cost of Canada's health-care system will not earn you any brownie points. Another conversational taboo would be to question someone's religious beliefs, since religion is seen as a strictly personal issue.

In fact, most controversial or derogatory remarks about social or cultural groups are taboo in Canada, particularly remarks about race, age, gender, or sexual orientation. This sensibility is reflected in the symbols used for public facilities and the choice of pronouns used with one's name. Thus James may identify as he/his, Julie as she/her, and Melida as they/them. Woke culture has taken some of these taboos to extremes: in 2014 the Toronto District School Board canceled a talk by Nobel Laureate Nadia Murad, an ISIS sex slave, as it could have been regarded as a promotion of Islamophobia.

Political affiliation is another example of asking the wrong question, as is curiosity about money and salaries in a personal conversation. Some political themes have become taboo, especially as a result of the pandemic and the pressure on Canadians to get vaccinated.

You can ask questions on just about any topic as long as it is done politely and respectfully; if you feel an uncomfortable edge to the conversation, simply change the subject.

CANADIAN HUMOR

Canadians do love a good laugh. Proof of this is the fact that Canada has the world's only postsecondary degree in writing and performing comedy (at Humber College

Twins dressed as harlequins in the Just for Laughs comedy festival in Montreal.

in Toronto), and the renowned French- and English-language festival Just for Laughs (Juste Pour Rire) in Montreal.

Canadians are immense fans of stand-up comedy. The national comedy club chain Yuk Yuk's has offered live, uncut comedy since it was started in the 1970s in Toronto by Mark Breslin and Jeff Silverman. Other comedy clubs are The Second City, the Corner Comedy Club, and the Comedy Bar.

However, it will come as no surprise that Canadian jokes tend to avoid laughing at or making fun of anyone. An exception to this politeness rule is Americans, especially the perception of American ignorance of Canada and Canadians. Other exceptions can be found in stand-up comedy, or in popular culture. Comedians like Indian–Canadian Russell Peters have become quite famous for their un-PC ethnic minority jokes, which run counter to the prevailing woke culture. Even wildly popular TV series like *Kim's Convenience* have been the target of many accusations of racism and cultural blunders.

There is also, in both French and English Canadian humor, a satirical tradition that targets social mores or beliefs. Recent examples from television include the political satires "This Hour Has 22 Minutes" and "Royal Canadian Air Farce," as well as "Les Bougons." They may seem rather serious and earnest, these Canadians, but they like having a good jab at their leaders—or at the Americans.

Fans of Hollywood comedies may not always be aware of the fact that some of their much-loved actors hail from Canada: the "Naked Gun" Leslie Nielsen, the "international man of mystery" Mike Myers, Jim Carrey "Ace Ventura", "the long shot" Seth Rogen, Tom Green, and many others. The original Canadian Broadcasting Corporation (CBC) sitcom "Schitt's Creek" (creators Eugene, Dan, and Fred Levy) stars Catherine O'Hara, Chris Elliot, Annie Murphy, Eugene and Dan Levy, and a myriad of talented Canadian comedians: it has become an absolute favorite among international audiences, having been shown on platforms such as Netflix since 2017, and breaking the record for most Emmy nominations (15) in its final season in 2020.

CHAPTER FIVE

AT HOME

LIVABLE CITIES

Three-quarters of the population live in cities, though there are only three very large cities: Montreal, Toronto, and Calgary. Even these are relatively small in comparison to American conglomerations, although in terms of population Toronto is the fourth-largest, and Montreal the eighth-largest city in North America. Canadian cities are compact, dynamic, and pleasant, and mix residences with commerce and services. Cities are places where people live, work, and play, a concept that is closer to the European urban model. They are very green, too—so much so that Toronto is called the "city in the park."

The Canadians' experience of daily life hints at the contradiction that the country is both a big place and a very small one. It is a vast area with a small population; it has large, modern cities with a small-town atmosphere. Aware of the expanse of their country, Canadians focus their energies on their homes, communities, and cities.

BIG VERSUS SMALL

There is a phenomenon of small towns that build big things to attract tourists—though it may also be a response to being a dot on the map of a huge country. Here are some examples:

- The world's largest *perogy* (Ukrainian dumpling) stands skewered on a fork in Glendon, Alberta (population 459). The fiberglass and steel *perogy* is 27 feet (8.2 m) high, 12 feet (3.7 m) wide, and weighs 6,000 pounds (2,722 kg).

- Moonbeam, Ontario (population around 1,200), is home to a large flying saucer (spaceship). It is 18 feet (5.5 m) in diameter and stands 9 feet (2.7 m) high.

- In Davidson, Saskatchewan (population around 1,000), locals have erected a 24 foot (7.3 m) high coffeepot and cup to highlight the friendliness and hospitality of the town.

- "Mr. Applehead," a 39 foot (12 m) tall by 37.7 foot (11.5 m) wide apple-shaped structure, is the tourist attraction near Colborne, a village in the municipality of Cramahe in Ontario. The eponymous Big Apple complex has a bakery (everything apple-related), a restaurant, an amusement park, picnic area, and a petting zoo (where visitors can touch and feed the animals).

Toronto, the "city in the park."

COMFORTABLE HOMES

Around two-thirds of Canadians own their own homes.
Of these, the vast majority live in single-family, detached
houses. In more crowded urban areas there are also row
houses, "duplexes" (two homes sharing one roof), and rental
apartment complexes. Condominiums (privately owned
apartments) are also popular in the larger cities—they are
the preferred residence of young professionals working
downtown, who like to be close to the office, shopping,
and entertainment. High-rise condominium buildings
are mostly located in the city center, and their number is
constantly growing, an example of vertical urbanization.

In Canada, size matters—heating costs during the
long winters mean that smaller houses make economic
sense. Homes are well insulated, well heated, and cozy in
the winter. Canadians are proud homeowners or renters,
maintaining their properties well. Flowers on porches

Suburban idyll. A well-appointed detached house in Montreal.

and perfectly trimmed lawns are a common sight in the summer.

And Canadians want comfort at home. Large, well-equipped kitchens are the norm, and are often the center of family activity. Any good party invariably ends up in the kitchen. There will be a family room, which might be called the TV room, den, study, or "rec room" (recreation room). Most detached houses have a semi-underground level, the basement, which may be used as a laundry room, workroom, for storage, or as a TV room or teenage hangout. Alternatively it may be rented out.

Canadians prefer showers to baths. To some visitors it may come as a surprise that everything (w.c., bath/shower) is in the same room. In Canada the w.c. is sometimes called the powder room. Also known as a half bath or guest bath, typically it only has a toilet and a basin and is located on the first floor of the house.

Detached homes generally have a front yard and backyard (or garden), and somewhere in the back there is probably a barbecue. Many yards are not delineated by fences. The property lines between homes may be nearly invisible, but everyone knows where they are. Canadians are strictly respectful of each other's space, and no one would dream of stepping into someone else's terrain uninvited—much less "borrow" the lawn chairs. Where people have pools (despite the long winters, summers are hot and plenty of people have them) these are often aboveground, this type being cheaper to install and easier to maintain. "Affordable and practical" is a trademark of other aspects of Canadian homes. For instance, the exterior of many homes is finished with a wood-lookalike vinyl product (vinyl siding) because it is cheaper than wood or brick and because it is maintenance free: it withstands the blizzards and cold as well as the hot summer sun and doesn't need to be painted.

Electricity is, as in the United States, 110–120 V, 60 Hz (or 500 V for heavy appliances, such as stoves). There are two common plug types: American-style with two parallel flat prongs above a circular grounding pin; or just two parallel flat prongs.

FAMILIES

Canadian society has traditionally been family-oriented in the sense that the family unit, however defined, is a cornerstone of social life. It is common, for instance, for

Young family on the campus of McGill University, Montreal.

families to take vacations together, all meeting at the cottage or someone's home for at least a part of their vacations. However, things are changing: families tend to be smaller—an average of 1.7 children throughout the country, a statistic that helps explain the immigration policy—and couples are waiting longer to have children. In 2021, of 10.5 million Canadian families 65 percent were still headed by two married parents, 19 percent were common-law arrangements (couples living without an official marriage), and 16 percent one-person households and single households (single parents and blended families where children from previous marriages are living together). In 2003 gay marriages were legalized and an increasing number of same-sex couples are raising children.

Meals in Canada are very much a part of family routine. Breakfast (a quick bowl of cereal or piece of toast) is generally eaten together. Children don't come home at lunchtime, taking a packed lunch (or perhaps having something in the cafeteria in secondary school). Most workers will bring a sandwich from home or have a quick bite out in their short lunch break from work. Many families try to eat dinner together, relatively early—around 6:00 or 7:00 p.m. Homework and TV-watching will fill many evenings throughout the year. An after-dinner walk around the block may be added to the schedule, especially on weekends. Another part of the routine is the weekly grocery shopping trip to one of the big store chains. Large refrigerators in homes permit this weekly stocking up. Visits to specialized shops for luxury items, like imported foods, or to the local farmers' market happen on weekends.

The Covid-19 pandemic changed food shopping habits overnight. In addition to the traditional takeout pizza dinners, demand for meal kits (boxes packed with portions of raw ingredients accompanied by a recipe for cooking at home) grew. Ordering food using apps such as Ritual, DoorDash, Foodora, SkipTheDishes (Canada's most popular food delivery app), and Little Caesars (the pizza ordering app, which has more than 5,000,000 users), and coffee shops like Tim Hortons became a part of everyday life in pandemic Canada.

One area that preoccupies Canadian families is the impact of dual-career parents on the upbringing of their children. Canadians work long hours and have very few holidays (see more in Chapter 7). The drop in the number of stay-at-home mothers happened quickly, and the impact on children is a major topic of public discourse as well as the subject of many studies, reports, articles, and debates. In 2016 around three-quarters of all mothers worked, around three-quarters of them full-time. The pandemic created additional problems for working parents: they had to combine their work-from-home responsibilities with the supervision of their online-studying children and the housework, food, and everything in between. This may have contributed to the fact that within two months (February to April 2020) 4.7 percent of women fell out of the labor force.

Generally, Canadian grandparents are not responsible for taking care of their grandchildren as more than 80 percent do not live together. Grandparents tend to enjoy their retirement years at home, their second home, or traveling. This is why children have to attend childcare centers, which are very expensive, especially the privately run ones.

Canadian families more often than not share household responsibilities, though it would be going too far to say that roles are apportioned equally. As in many other countries, women still take on the larger part of the housework and child-rearing duties. Canadian women, like their peers in other developed countries, complain of the stress of their busy lives, especially those combining careers and child-rearing.

Childcare Issues

The cost of raising a child in Canada is quite high: Can$10,000 to Can$15,000 a year until they turn eighteen. Canada has no national program or policy for childcare except for specific programs for Indigenous, military, and newcomer families; this is why the national agreement in March 2022 to contribute a subsidy of Can$8 dollars a day toward childcare for low-income families is considered a major step in this direction.

For working mothers across the country, the issue of childcare is a major preoccupation in terms of cost and availability. For young children between eighteen months and five years, the demand for childcare outstrips the supply of services. Around one-half of all children in this age group are in some form of day care, mostly in institutionally organized facilities. Most of these are private, commercial centers. The number of government-supported day-care services (covering only 20 percent of demand) is way below the average for Western Europe.

In 2022, the provincial government of Quebec established a subsidy of Can$8.35 a day for day care; this, however only meets 20 percent of the demand. At a non-subsidized day-care service, the daily fees can range from Can$35 to Can$60. Elsewhere, childcare is generally treated as a private responsibility, one between family demand and private sector supply. The federal government today is wary of establishing the large and costly bureaucracy that would be necessary to run a public care system. Instead, the government provides financial support for families with children under the age of six.

The need for childcare services doesn't end when a child starts school, so there is a network of before-school and after-school programs for the six-to-twelve-year age group that is also primarily offered through the private sector. Many of these take place in school buildings. The phenomenon of latchkey children—those who spend afternoons alone at home (or in a public library)—first arose in the 1980s, when mothers joined the workforce in large numbers. The Covid-19 pandemic created a new generation of latchkey kids overnight as after-school programs were canceled, or reduced in number, increasing prices.

SUMMER CAMPS AND THE WORK ETHIC

Then there are the summer vacations. Primary and secondary schoolchildren have up to three months of summer vacations, while their parents have only two or three weeks a year. This has given rise to a very large "camp" industry: day camps, residential camps, camps focused on sports, outdoor experiences, science, language, creative arts, museums . . . they all thrive. Young children attend these camps, and older girls and boys run them. This system gives teenagers a large source of summer jobs, useful not only for the money, but also for the skills and experience that they can put on their curricula vitae.

The work ethic begins early with Canadians: almost half of all secondary schoolchildren have paid work. For girls this is most often babysitting, and for the younger boys it is a newspaper delivery route. Older teenagers work in restaurants or in the retail sector. For those who frown at this "abuse" of the carefree years of youth, statistics indicate that students who don't work at all are more likely to drop out of high school than those who have jobs. On the other hand, high school students who concentrate more on their jobs than on their schooling are most likely to drop out—there is obviously a fine line to be drawn here. University students have four months off in the summer; every one of them has a summer job, and many also hold part-time jobs during the year to help make ends meet.

Covid-19 and Life at Home

The Covid-19 pandemic changed everything: with the start of the lockdowns in early 2020, millions of office workers and all school-age children and college and university students stayed home and switched their activities online; but this was just the beginning of sweeping changes for Canadians. The home-based work/study lifestyle had to be adopted literally overnight, and not everyone was happy. People suddenly realized they needed more space to coexist and not be in the way of other family members. Many sold their downtown condos or left their rented apartments and moved out of the city, either returning to their parents' home or investing in larger accommodation in suburbia, or even farther away. Real estate prices exploded, and house affordability sank. A family with two working parents and two students needed four workstations, and the adults had to take on all household duties in addition to supervising their online-studying kids. The closure of summer camps left working parents struggling with their children's activities. Single adults felt isolated without the physical contact they'd previously enjoyed with friends and coworkers. Many adopted pets, or became socially active on social media platforms such as LinkedIn, Reddit, and Instagram, and started dating online. Many new niche dating apps appeared in addition to the well-established ones such as Tinder, Bumble, Badoo, and the popular Canadian Plenty of Fish: Elite Singles, eharmony, Canadian Friends Date, Lovestruck, and Maple Match, among others. Millions of people signed up to find new friends and dates, and meet new people.

For others, the stress of their financial situation, the changes to daily routines, separation from friends, and worries about the health of family members resulted in mental health deterioration and an increase in substance use and abuse.

EDUCATION

Canadians are, on the whole, highly educated.
- More than 61 percent of adults aged 25 to 64 have a postsecondary qualification.
- Around 38.6 percent have a university degree and 22.4 percent have a trades certificate.

- Around 25 percent have only a high school diploma; fewer than 14 percent have no certificate.
- A small percent of primary and secondary schools are private (most are denominational).
- More than two hundred postgraduate institutions of various types exist across the country.

Thirteen Different Systems

There is one important particularity in the Canadian education system: it is a provincial responsibility. This means that there are thirteen education systems that reflect local history, culture, and educational priorities. The Ministry of Education in each province and territory sets standards and curriculum guidelines, and provides financial support to schools. The schools are administered through elected school boards, which set budgets, hire teachers, and further define the curriculum.

The Canadian education system is generally seen as being progressive and liberal, stressing individual thought and stimulating a desire to learn. Given the lack of central coordination, however, how does the country manage to maintain a uniformly good reputation for its education system? There are variations in standards at all levels of the education program, from one institution to another as well as from one province or territory to another. However, the variations in Canada are nowhere near as large as those between schools and universities in the USA. A certain coordination of standards is achieved by several means, including regular international and Canadian studies that compare the levels of student attainment, providing benchmarks for schools to make adjustments. Also, a measure of provincial/territorial cooperation is achieved through the regular meetings of the Council of Ministers of Education.

Primary and Secondary Education

Children are required to attend school from six or seven years of age until fifteen or sixteen, depending on the province or territory. A majority of students graduate from high school after twelve years, at the age of eighteen or nineteen. There are schools that provide a more practical high school degree leading on to technical programs, but most children follow the regular high school program whether they go on to university or not.

The exception is the system in Quebec, where children complete eleven years of high school. They then attend a CEGEP (*collège d'enseignement général et professionnel*, or professional and general education college), which provides two-year preuniversity programs or three-year technical or vocational programs.

Primary and secondary education are free in public schools. "Separate" schools are public denominational schools, the majority of which are Roman Catholic. There are also a few private schools that are totally independent and offer a variety of curricula based on religion, language, or academic abilities. Quebec has the highest proportion of children attending private schools in Canada and the USA.

Graduation day at Simon Fraser University in Burnaby, Greater Vancouver.

Universities and Colleges

Postsecondary institutions include universities, community colleges, technical colleges, university colleges, and career colleges.

Universities provide academic degrees. They are publicly funded but are autonomous in setting their own admission standards and study requirements.

Community colleges and technical institutes provide vocational training diplomas. They are unique internationally in that they aim primarily to respond to the training needs of business, industry, and the public-service sector. Annual tuition fees for these in 2022 were Can$4,000 for Canadians and up to Can$18,000 for international students.

University colleges do a bit of both, in that they offer both degrees and diplomas.

Career colleges, which are privately owned and managed (though they are approved and regulated by

The Romanesque Revival-style building of University College, Toronto.

the provincial authorities), provide job-specific, short-term training.

For Canadian university students, fees (which the government likes to remind people cover only around 20 percent of the total cost) average around Can$8,000 per year. These vary by province, university, degree, program of study, and so on. The lowest fees are in Quebec, where they are less than half the national average; the highest are in Nova Scotia. The debt burden carried by graduates looms large in the public debate today. Students use a mix of government-supported student loan programs, part-time jobs, scholarships, and family support to cover the costs of fees, books, and living expenses. A growing number of students choose to live at home in order to keep costs down.

Foreign Students

Studying in Canada is more expensive than in Europe, but less expensive than in the USA. For foreign students, however, it is important to note that there are different fee structures: lowest for students who are from the same province; higher for Canadian students from other provinces; and highest for foreign students.

Canada is a popular study destination. In pre-pandemic 2019, there were 638,380 international students studying at all levels of the Canadian system. Their number went down sharply the following year, rebounding to pre-pandemic levels and reaching 621,565 in 2021. More than half of these were from Asian countries: India, China, South Korea, the Philippines, Bangladesh, Japan, and Vietnam. Most students report having good experiences in terms of the quality of the education they received and their experience of living in Canada. International students are attracted by the tolerant and welcoming atmosphere of the country and the opportunity to stay and work, thanks to the PGWP (postgraduate work permit) program. They can also work while studying, thus getting Canadian work experience, supporting themselves financially, and learning a lot about the economy, culture, and way of life there. Because of the numbers of foreign students, there are often special programs for them, such as homestays (where a student stays with a Canadian family for a few days before the start of their school term), and organized meetings with foreign and Canadian students. A mass of information is available on all aspects of studying in Canada on the Web; just set an evening aside and type in "study in Canada."

CHAPTER SIX

TIME OUT

Canadians are busy, even in their free time. They are big shoppers, spending lots of time at the mall, and put a great deal of time and energy into fixing their homes and cottages. They enjoy the outdoors and the many festivals in their community, are sporty and active, love going out to restaurants and cinemas, but are equally happy to "veg out" in front of the television. There is a huge range of leisure activities available, from enjoying the breathtaking natural environment and the multitude of sports facilities, to shopping and visiting museums. The other wonderful thing is that all of these activities are accessible to everyone, and obtaining information about the activity of your choice is easy.

CANADIANS ON VACATION

From May to October it is not unusual to see a weekend exodus from the cities to the countryside, where many

Canadians have cottages. A Canadian cottage can be anything from a fully-fledged second home to a wooden shack beside a lake or river full of fish, and if you don't own one you can rent one. Information can be obtained from Web sites and tourist information bureaus. If you have the good fortune of being invited to someone's cottage, it will be a great chance to see the countryside, and to watch your host unwind—while mowing the lawn, fixing the cottage and the boat, and preparing food for the numerous houseguests.

For those who can afford it, Canadians also fly south at some point in the year to get a full dose of sunshine and vitamin D. Florida and the Caribbean islands are popular hot spots. Europe is also a destination for those looking for cultural input, but most charter flights go south.

After the outbreak of the Covid-19 pandemic and the imposition of various restrictions on travel and movement, the vast majority of Canadians reported spending less or nothing at all on at least one of the following: short-term rentals, or domestic or international travel. From October 2021 it became impossible for unvaccinated Canadians to leave the country, or even board a domestic flight, train, or bus. After August 2022 foreign nationals weren't able to board a flight or train in order to leave Canada unless they were vaccinated. In a word, in the aftermath of vaccination mandates, restrictions, and the like, the post-pandemic world was starkly different. Pandemic measures were eased in early 2022, and to increase expenditure on leisure and travel, provincial governments started encouraging travel within the provinces by offering tax credits on certain travel-related expenses, while discouraging other types of travel such as cruise ship vacations and warning against travel in many countries. Then, in May 2022, monkeypox cases in North America and Europe raised new fears.

The Great Outdoors

Canada has thirty-nine national parks, a thousand provincial parks, fifty territorial parks, and more than eight hundred national historical sites. Some of the parks are as large as small countries. In these areas, a huge variety of activities are available, from camping, hiking, mountain climbing, and fishing in the summer, to downhill and cross-country skiing, ice fishing, and dogsledding in the winter. You don't have to be an intrepid canoe camper, disappearing for days in the wild with a tent and a bag of food, to enjoy this wilderness: there are RV (mobile home) parks with washing facilities and gas and electricity outlets.

It's a Long, Long Road

The Trans-Canada Trail is the world's longest, shared-use recreational trail. It is 10,004 miles (16,100 km) long, and crosses all the provinces and territories. It is used for walking, cycling, horseback riding, cross-country skiing, and snowmobiling.

Hiking in the spectacular Howe Sound, northwest of Vancouver.

Courses are available for those who would like to try something new, such as rock climbing, and there are guides or group arrangements for those who want to experience the great outdoors but who don't want to take it on alone. All equipment can be rented, from tents to RVs, with a barbecue thrown in if you like— for a price, of course.

Many Canadians love their natural environment and make use of it frequently: every year there are around sixteen million visits to the country's national parks. Add to this the number of Canadians who own a rural summerhouse, and the many visits to other nature areas, such as provincial, territorial, or city parks, and one sees a pattern of intense use. City parks, for instance, are the favorite place for ethnic community members—in social groups or extended families— whose collectivist culture engages some in group games and competitions while others prepare the food and take care of the children. However, not all Canadians are nature lovers; there are devout urbanites who don't relish Canada's ever-present natural forces (cold and snow in the winter, heat and bugs in the summer). Many young adults belong to board game clubs; others engage in activities such as speed socializing events where they meet other like-minded people for dating, friendship, and even business. While a majority of Canadians are aware of and concerned by environmental issues, their affluent way of life is as polluting as that of America. The biggest difference is that, with a larger territory and much smaller population, the effects are perhaps less visible.

Being Prepared

Canadians are well equipped for whatever activity they choose to engage in. Good equipment is part of being prepared for the worst; the great outdoors in Canada is vast and wild, with no handily placed pubs or first-aid centers. Here are a few things to consider:

- High season is in July and August, when the most popular parks (those closest to urban areas) are crowded, especially on weekends. Reservations may be necessary, and be prepared for traffic jams out of the cities and on entering the parks.
- Bugs, particularly flying things that sting, are abundant in the summer, especially in June and July. Mosquitoes and midges (which bite mainly from sunset on), and black flies and horseflies (which bite during the day) are good examples.

- Check the weather forecast for the area to be visited.
- Bring all the proper gear, including water, or iodine purification tablets if you are planning to get water from rivers or lakes (there may be upstream pollution).

SPORTS

Canadians enjoy many sports, most of which are easily accessible to visitors, either as spectators or as participants. Ice hockey is the great national obsession, and tickets to watch ice hockey games of the National Hockey League are in great demand. Some famous hockey players whose names you should know, in order to impress your Canadian friends over a beer, are Mario Lemieux, Wayne Gretzky, Gordie Howe, and Maurice Richard. Children will play hockey in the street, in local indoor and outdoor rinks, and on any frozen surface large enough for two or more players. Visitors tempted to join them in a neighborhood game should be warned—these children are as comfortable on skates as they are in running shoes.

Curling is another popular organized sport in winter. The Canadian Curling Association estimates that there are 1,100 affiliated clubs, fourteen provincial and territorial associations, and well over a million Canadians who play the sport on a regular basis.

The most popular summer sport is baseball. Canada has its own version of football, which is slightly different

Fly fishing at sunrise in the pristine wilderness.

from the American game and not to be confused with soccer.

In addition to ice hockey, lacrosse is one of Canada's national sports, though it is only played by select groups, mainly in the western provinces. It is North America's oldest organized sport, invented by the Algonquin Indians from the St. Lawrence valley region.

For keeping fit there are gyms and health clubs in all cities and towns, from ritzy private centers to inexpensive YMCA facilities. Tennis, squash, and racquetball are also often available. The most popular participant sports in Canada are swimming (in indoor and outdoor pools), hiking, cycling, jogging, golf, skiing, and fishing. In winter, most urban areas will have places for ice-skating and tobogganing in local parks. It isn't unusual to see people cross-country skiing or snowshoeing in city parks for exercise.

ON ICE

Ottawa has the world's largest skating rink on the Rideau Canal: a path of 4.85 miles (7.8 km) and averaging 148 feet (45 m) in width is maintained each winter. However, in 2008 Winnipeg created the world's longest skating rink, with a 6.6 to 9.8 foot-wide (2 to 3 m), 5.25 mile-long (8.45 km) skating path on the Assiniboine and Red Rivers.

Children playing ice hockey on a frozen lake in Banff National Park, Alberta.

FESTIVALS

There are hundreds of festivals year round across the country, many of them free. Some are as simple as street music performance, while others celebrate specific aspects of the local culture or history of the province or territory. Yet others have a specific theme, such as music or literature, and most are of high quality. Some cater to the local population, and others are internationally renowned; all are fun and make for a good time out. The International Film Festivals in Toronto, Vancouver, and Montreal, Calgary's Reggaefest, Scotiabank Caribbean Carnival Toronto, Charlottetown's Jazz and Blues Festival, and Montreal's Jazz Festival are all well-known.

Internationally known summer events include the **Calgary Stampede**, a festival, exhibition, and rodeo held over ten days in the second week of July. It is one of Canada's largest annual events, and the world's largest outdoor rodeo. In Newfoundland and Labrador, the **Royal St. John's Regatta** is North America's oldest continuous sporting event, documented since 1826. It is scheduled for the first Wednesday of August, but if the weather is unsuitable the event is postponed until the next suitable day. The Regatta Day is an official holiday in the province, and the decision to go ahead or not generates an amazing amount of public interest. **Highland Games** take place in several cities in Nova Scotia in July and celebrate its Scottish heritage and links between the old world and the new. Yukon's **International Storytelling Festival** takes place every

Bucking bronco competition at the Calgary Stampede.

summer in Whitehorse, bringing together writers and storytellers from around the world.

If you are visiting Canada in the winter, try to schedule your trip to coincide with one of the many winter festivals. It is a great way to see how best to take advantage of the cold weather. Winter festivals include the **Carnaval de Quebec** in Quebec City, the world's largest winter festival and the third largest of any type of festival, after the carnivals in Rio and New Orleans. It takes place over seventeen days in January and/or February. It celebrates the joys of winter with ice sculpture competitions, sled dog races, outdoor dance parties, and legendary parades. For the very brave there are canoe races on the frozen St. Lawrence River (which basically consists of teams running over the ice alongside their canoes) and the annual snow bath, where people in bathing suits wash up with clean snow. **Winterlude** is Ottawa's winter festival. It takes place during three weekends in February, taking advantage of the city's canal, which, as we've seen, is the largest ice-skating rink in the world. It features free daily outdoor concerts, snow- and ice-sculpture competitions, and a playground made of snow that includes thirty giant snow slides. The **Festival du Voyageur** in Winnipeg, Manitoba, celebrates the history of Canada's fur trade period. The many historical and family-oriented activities take place during ten days in February. There is a torchlight walk, a fiddling and jigging contest, competitive games that include leg wrestling, tug of war, and log sawing, and the Governor's Ball, for which guests dress in nineteenth-century costume, enjoy a five-course meal, and dance. Many activities take place at Fort Gibraltar, a reconstruction of the original fort that was at the center of fur trading.

The **Cabane-à-sucre**, or **Sugar Bush**, is not an official festival, but the arrival of spring in the provinces of Ontario, Quebec, and the four Atlantic Provinces means fresh sources of maple syrup, making a visit to the local sugar bush a must. A sugar bush is an area where enough maple trees grow to collect sap to make maple syrup. In the spring, many maple farms are open to the public and give presentations on the traditions of collecting and making maple syrup, a tradition that European settlers learned from the Native Peoples. This day out also includes a large meal with copious quantities of fresh maple syrup. Walks or a sleigh ride through the forest make it a lovely family outing.

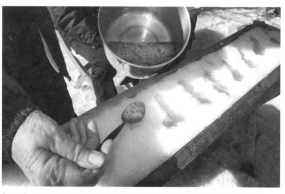

Spreading maple syrup on snow to make toffee at a sugar shack in Quebec.

Contemporary carved totem pole in Stanley Park, Vancouver.

OTHER ENTERTAINMENT

All of Canada's provincial capitals and most cities have theaters (both professional and amateur theater thrives), nightclubs, museums, and art galleries. World-class entertainment choices range from ballet, opera, and classical music to internationally famous rock and pop acts. In art galleries, the Group of Seven (a group of famous contemporary Canadian painters) and Native Indian art are two particularly Canadian forms to look out for. Some of Canada's museums are relatively new constructions and are thus modern and innovative in their approach to presenting and displaying their collections. Some of the hands-on science centers are good examples of this.

Music
Canada's popular music industry is booming, in both English- and French-language spheres. Some famous

Free jazz concert in the park, Verdun, Montreal.

Canadian singers (often mistakenly assumed to be American) include the doyen of singer-songwriters Leonard Cohen, folk and rock stars Gordon Lightfoot, Neil Young, and Bryan Adams, and pop icons Joni Mitchell, Anne Murray, Celine Dion, Shania Twain, and Alanis Morissette. Canadian rock bands The Guess Who, Rash, The Tragically Hip, and The Barenaked Ladies have all made great contributions to the world of rock and roll. Twenty-first-century Canadian pop music boasts mainstream Canadian artists with global record sales and international recording contracts such as Diana Kroll, Michael Bublé, Feist, Nelly Furtado, Deadmau5, Avril Lavigne, Drake, and Justin Bieber, who have achieved international success and dominated the North American music charts.

There is an active classical music scene in Canada that includes orchestras, opera companies, and ballet companies. Performances by international artists provide extra variety to the yearly program.

Cinema

Going to the cinema in Canada is much like going to the movies in the United States. Only 5 percent of the films shown are "made in Canada," and the majority are of the Hollywood blockbuster type. Finding a selection of European films in the commercial film houses is difficult. Canadian films have won Oscars and recognition at the Cannes Film Festival. The Quebecois fim industry has done well in international circles with such box office successes as Denys Arcand's *The Decline of the American Empire* and *The Barbarian Invasions* (which won an Oscar as best foreign language film), as have several animated films and documentaries. Other French-Canadian directors such as Atom Egoyan and Denis Villeneuve have been awarded the highest prizes in the industry.

"Saturday Night Live" producer Lorne Michaels is Canadian, as is James Cameron, the director of numerous mega blockbusters—*Terminator*, *Rambo*, *Titanic*, and *Avatar*. David Cronenberg, the director of *The Fly* and *History of Violence*, also hails from Canada. There is no doubt that the North American film scene is indebted to Canadian talent at many levels.

Canadian actors, such as film legend Mary Pickford, working in Hollywood in the early days of the twentieth century contributed to the creation of the Canadian motion picture industry. Among notable Canadian actors are Lorne Greene, William Shatner, Michael J. Fox, Donald Sutherland, Christopher Plummer, Ryan Gosling, Ryan Reynolds, Pamela Anderson, Rachel

McAdams, and Elliot (Ellen) Page. Canada's contribution to North American comedy may exceed its contribution to dramatic acting. Jim Carrey, Mike Myers (Austin Powers), Samantha Bee, Catherine O'Hara, Dan Akroyd, Tommy Chong, and the late John Candy, Phil Hartmann, and Leslie Nielsen are all Canadian.

EATING OUT

Canadians love to go out for dinner, lunch, or breakfast, and for weekend brunches (combining a late breakfast with an early lunch). There are restaurants catering to every budget, from cheap fast food and affordable family diners to hip cafés and expensive restaurants. One of the great pleasures of living in a multicultural country is the variety of cuisines brought by immigrants, and the opportunity to sample exotic foods without having to travel to faraway lands.

When in Vancouver try the Indian and Chinese restaurants. In Calgary the local beef is simply amazing. Toronto offers food from around the world—Afghan, Belgian, Caribbean, Chinese, Iranian, Mediterranean, Turkish, Middle Eastern, Mexican, Brazilian, Thai, Filipino, Vietnamese. You name it, they have it. Montreal, boasting the highest number of restaurants per capita in Canada, is a treasure island of ethnic cuisines—Cambodian, Ethiopian, Portuguese, Italian, Australian, Ukrainian, British, Pakistani, Middle Eastern, Polish, Korean, Colombian. It is perfectly

Outdoor restaurant in Quebec's Place Royale.

possible to eat out for months without going to the same restaurant twice.

Dining out is generally a relaxed affair. In much of English-speaking Canada etiquette resembles American norms; Quebec is more French. Water is served (free) at every meal, usually with ice, and coffee may be ordered to accompany your food—it is a Canadian quirk to drink coffee while eating lunch. But there are no hard and fast rules. Friends going out together will usually split the bill.

There are some homegrown fast-food places that have become part of the local lingo. Tim Hortons is for light lunches, donuts, and especially coffee (though for Europeans Canadian coffee may be a bit of a letdown). St-Hubert BBQ is Quebec's answer to Kentucky Fried Chicken but is way better and far healthier! Laura Secord is a well-known chocolate shop.

TYPICAL CANADIAN FOODS

- Maple syrup comes from maple sap, which is collected and processed by methods handed down from the Native Peoples to the first European settlers. Eighty percent of the world's maple syrup comes from Canada, of which 90 percent is from Quebec. Syrup is graded according to color, flavor, and density, Grade A being the best.
- Beaver Tails: a pancakelike fried snack coated in sugar.
- Poutine: French fries, gravy, and cheese curds, with an optional sausage (you don't have to be born there to like it!).
- Smoked meat sandwiches in Montreal delis.
- Lobster on the east coast, salmon on the west coast, and trout from every river.
- Lumberjack's breakfast, aka logger's breakfast, aka "The Lumby"—a gargantuan breakfast of three-plus eggs, rations of ham, bacon, and sausages, and several large pancakes. Invented by the hotelier J. Houston around 1870 at his Granville Hotel on Water Street in old pre-railway Gastown, Vancouver.
- Vancouver Nanaimo bars: a non-bake dessert named after the city in British Columbia. The creamy, custardy center is what sets Nanaimo bars apart from the buttercream-filled New

York slice—both have a smooth chocolate topping and a rich Graham cracker crust.

- The Caesar, often called Canada's national cocktail. A proud Calgary invention, this was the brainchild of Italian-born bartender Walter Chell. Legend has it that in 1969 he adapted his beloved pasta with clam sauce into this zesty tomato-clam juice cocktail spiked with vodka.
- The Donair, a unique Canadian version of the döner kebab from Halifax, which features a distinctive sauce made from condensed milk, sugar, garlic, and vinegar.

DRINKING

The minimum age for drinking in Canada is eighteen or nineteen, depending on the province or territory. In most areas, bars close around 1:00 or 2:00 a.m., except in Quebec, where they stay open until 3:00 or 4:00 a.m. Drunkenness is not viewed kindly in Canada, unless you are a student, and drunk driving is a serious offense.

The most popular alcoholic drink in Canada is beer. Canadians pride themselves on the fact that their beer is both tastier and stronger than American beer. It is generally served very cold, and there is a greater variety of labels than in the USA, though fewer than in, say, Belgium. The two biggest beer producers in Canada are Molson and Labatt, but a whole series of microbreweries increases the range of tastes on the Canadian market. In recent years, though, wine has become the first choice of drink, leaving domestic and imported beers in second and third place. Excellent Canadian wines are made in Ontario and British Columbia, and the former is the global ice wine leader.

Canadian Joke

American beer is like making love in a canoe. They are both very close to water.

The sale of alcoholic beverages in Canada is government controlled and highly taxed, and they are therefore expensive. Canadian beer is the most affordable (imports are more expensive). Imported wine is very expensive (in European terms). Alcoholic beverages can only be purchased in separate liquor stores called Liquor Control Boards (the Société des Alcools du Québec, or SAQ in Quebec) and in provinces like Ontario beer can also only be bought in separate beer stores. The exception is in Quebec, where beer and wine are also available in any grocery store or *dépanneur* (convenience store). Quality and choice will be limited here, however.

You will probably hear Canadians talk about a "two-four" or a "crate." They both mean twenty-four bottles or cans of beer.

TIPPING
....

Waiters and waitresses, hairdressers, barbers, and taxi drivers in Canada depend on tips for a large proportion of their earnings—their wages are not high. Leaving a tip, unless the service has been truly appalling, is therefore vital. It should be around 15 percent of the (pretax) bill, or a little less or more depending on how you feel about the service. In places such as hotels, airports, and other ports of travel, porters or bellhops are usually paid Can$2–5 per item of luggage they carry.

SMOKING

Smoking in Canada is basically out of fashion. Fewer than 20 percent of all Canadians still smoke, and they are restricted from doing so in most public spaces across the country (though provincial legislation varies). If you are a smoker, you will be expected to ask the people around you whether they mind if you smoke, even if you are in a place where it is allowed.

In October 2018 Canada became the second country in the world, and the first of the G7, to legalize cannabis for recreational purposes (it had been made legal to use it for medicinal purposes seventeen years earlier). This came with regulations restricting home production and distribution, as well as places of sale and usage. Cannabis laws vary from province to province, and cannabis products cannot yet be promoted or advertised nationwide.

Single Issue Politics

The Marijuana Party of Canada is a federal political party established in 2000 whose sole focus is on cannabis-related issues in the country. Other than that, its members are free to express their views on other political matters according to their convictions.

SHOPPING

As in the United States, shopping in malls is not only a means of purchasing things one needs, it is also a pastime. Malls are large, practical (especially when it is cold outside), provide good and free parking, and have a wide range of products on offer. However, most cities and even neighborhoods also have their shopping street to meet local needs, and city centers are generally full of shops selling products that are not available in the malls. The larger department stores and chains also have shops in the city centers.

The majority of stores, shops, and supermarkets in Canada are open from at least 9:00 a.m. until 5:30 p.m., and there is always a pharmacist and grocery store open twenty-four hours a day. Shops and grocery stores are open across the country on Sundays, though there are provincial differences in opening hours. Large supermarket chains such as Metro and Walmart are open from 7:00 a.m. to 11:00 p.m. on workdays and 9:00 a.m. to 6:00 p.m. on national holidays.

The Covid-19 pandemic hit commerce hard: malls closed, and shops were allowed to sell only if they could offer curbside pickup. This caused a strong shift to online shopping: numerous apps appeared, and there was a rapid growth in the second-hand market because of heightened environmental consciousness, the need to save, and financial savvy. Many people started side businesses on the Canadian e-commerce platform Shopify, the American Etsy, and Amazon. At the same time, an anti-Amazon trend grew and developed, giving rise to direct-to-consumer business models such as drop-shipping, and cashless payment solutions like the Square app, Paypal, and others.

Shop and Hop

The West Edmonton Mall in Alberta covers forty-eight city blocks and contains shops, the world's largest indoor amusement park, and the highest indoor bungee jump.

CHAPTER SEVEN

TRAVEL, HEALTH, & SAFETY

Travel in Canada, whether getting around locally or going across the country, is generally pleasant, safe, and practical. The infrastructure and services are of high quality, and information about options, conditions, and timetables is readily available. Most accommodation, attractions, and transportation systems are also accessible to people with physical disabilities. There are, however, fewer public transportation services in rural areas, so having a car is essential. Distances, even within Canadian cities, may surprise some visitors—make sure you plan properly, whether using public transportation networks or private cars. The metric system is used everywhere in Canada, including, for instance, in the signs indicating speed limits.

A good source of information on transportation issues generally is the Web site www.travelcanada.ca.

Streetcars on King Street in Toronto.

URBAN TRAVEL

Public Transportation

Although cars are by far the favorite mode of transportation in Canada, every city and town in the country has a reasonable and efficient public transportation system. Timetables, costs, and modes of transportation vary from place to place, and information is locally available or on the Internet. Buses are the most common form of transportation, but some cities also have trams, ferries, metros, and trains, all of which are clean and safe.

Water taxi in Victoria Inner Harbour, British Columbia.

Tickets for services are generally available on board any form of public transit, and are usually valid for the whole system, so you can use a combination of bus and tram or metro, for instance. You can also buy various types of tickets, such as one-time use, multiple use, or passes for longer periods of frequent use, from stations or designated shops (often newsstands). When purchasing tickets for one trip, it is wise to make sure you have ample small change, as change is not given.

In Toronto, tickets, tokens, and passes are no longer available at subway stations; passengers need a pre-paid PRESTO card, or exact change to get their ticket on the bus. There are fare vending machines at the entrances of all subway stations. Quebec has the OPUS card, utilized the same way as PRESTO.

Driving

Canada is second, after the USA, in the numbers of cars owned per person. Despite the number of cars on the roads, there are relatively few traffic accidents. This is in part due to the Canadian obsession with prevention. Traffic is highly regulated and rules are strictly enforced. Generally, driving on Canadian roads is pretty straightforward, though there are a few peculiarities that are useful to know.

Pedestrians have the right of way on Canadian roads, even when jaywalking (crossing a road anywhere other than at a crosswalk). If a pedestrian is on the road, don't just slow down—STOP! Failing to do so could land you with a hefty fine (and Canadians lose points on their driver's license). If a school bus, which is big, yellow, and clearly marked, has red lights flashing, drivers on both sides of the road must stop. This is to safeguard any child making a mad dash across the road.

Winter is hard on Canada's roads, creating potholes more rapidly than in warmer countries. Major repairs can only be undertaken in the snow-free summer months, which means that roads are frequently blocked, either by snow removal trucks or by repair teams. Most Canadian cities (except some of the older centers like Quebec City) are designed on a grid that is fairly easy to navigate, except where one-way systems can make getting to your destination more roundabout than may seem necessary.

BASIC RULES

- Drive on the right-hand side of the road.
- Wearing a seat belt is compulsory, even in the backseat.
- Cars in most provinces and territories must have their lights on during the day.
- In every province, except parts of Quebec (notably on Montreal Island), it is legal to make a right turn at a red traffic light after coming to a full stop, and when it is safe to do so, unless there is a sign that says "No Turn on Red."
- In British Columbia, a slow-flashing green light means you can go, but the light may change if a pedestrian pushes a button to cross the road.
- In Ontario and Quebec, a fast-flashing green light means the driver can make a left turn across oncoming traffic because oncoming traffic has a red light.
- Speed limit signs are in metric (kilometers).
- Driving under the influence of alcohol (called drunk driving) is very seriously enforced in Canada. In most provinces and territories the limit for blood alcohol level is 0.08 percent.

Most intersections in cities are protected, either with stop signs, yield signs, or traffic lights. (At stop signs you really are expected to stop, even if there is no one in sight; not quite stopping is called a rolling stop, and if you are seen by a police officer you will get a ticket.) For Europeans this will all seem a bit overprotective, but there you have it.

Of all Canadian drivers, Montrealers have the worst reputation for fast and aggressive driving. Also, throughout Quebec, most road signs are in French.

Tourists and visitors to Canada (except those from the USA) are advised to get an International Driving Permit from their home country in order to rent a car.

Starting from Cold!

Canadian cars are equipped with engine heaters that keep the engine oil from freezing when parked outside during winter. Snow removal trucks push the snow from the street to the side of the road. Cars parked along the sidewalks will therefore be covered in hard-packed snow, which will require serious shoveling to get free. Also, the snow removal action blocks driveways, which then also need shoveling. When leaving in the morning, all this shoveling, plus warming up the car, and defrosting the windows, needs to be planned for. Then don't forget that tires that have spent the night in freezing temperatures will develop a flat spot; one needs to drive slowly until the air in the tires has warmed up.

Taxis waiting for hire in downtown Toronto.

Taxis

In most cities taxis are plentiful and not too expensive. They can be hailed on the street, at a taxi center, or from a stand outside places such as hotels or train stations. Prices should be displayed inside the cab, though you may be expected to pay additional costs such as tolls (there are not many in the country) or surcharges at night or on Sundays. A tip of around 10 percent for good and friendly service is customary.

Ride-hailing apps are popular in Canada, the two main providers being Uber and Lyft. In addition, Uber Eats offers door-to-door food delivery services, while Lyft offers vehicle hire, free-floating electric scooters, and a bicycle-sharing system.

CROSS-COUNTRY TRAVEL

The good news is that there are many ways to get from one city to another in Canada. Which mode of transportation you use will be determined by how much time you have to spare, and how much money you want to spend.

Time Zones

The first thing to note about traveling across the country is that there are six time zones, each of one hour difference except for Newfoundland, which is a half hour ahead of the rest of the country.

Every Canadian knows a funny story about a European who wants to have breakfast in Quebec City, lunch in Toronto, and dinner in Vancouver, or some variation on the theme. Most people know Canada is a big place, but are still shocked when they realize just how long it takes to get from one place to another. For some, it takes a whole change in mind-set to get used to the distances.

It is also important to remember that most of Canada turns its clocks ahead one hour for Daylight Saving Time on the second Sunday in March. On the first Sunday in November the clocks are turned back an hour to Standard Time. The saying to help one remember whether the clock goes backward or forward is "fall back, spring forward." The only exception is Saskatchewan, which does not use Daylight Saving Time.

The Trans-Canada Highway at Banff, with Mount Bourgeau in the backgound.

Highways

The Trans-Canada Highway, which starts at Victoria
in British Columbia and crosses Canada to St. John's,
Newfoundland, is the world's longest highway, at
4,860 miles (7,821 km). Between cities the highways are
generally in good condition. Near urban areas they will be
multilane, but there are long stretches of single-lane road
with occasional extra lanes to allow passing. On most
of the country's highways the speed limit is 62 miles per
hour (100 kmph). Ontario introduced a higher limit of
68.4 miles per hour (110 kmph) on its 400-series
highways, including the Queen Elizabeth Way highway,
in spring 2022. The Weather Network provides

Overpass for wildlife on the Trans-Canada Highway.

constant road condition updates on its Web site, theweathernetwork.ca/roads, as well as on television and radio broadcasts.

Buses

The cheapest way to travel across Canada using public transportation is by motor coach (the North American term for a long-haul bus). The bus network is more extensive than the rail network, and the service more frequent than the trains.

Tickets cannot be purchased on the buses—they must be bought at a ticket office or bus terminal. The two largest companies were Greyhound (generally active from Toronto westward) and Voyageur Colonial (covering everything to the east, and owned by Greyhound). After operating in Canada for nearly a century, Greyhound Lines ended all bus services in Canada in May 2021, signaling the end of the bus line age. Since then bus services have been provided by VIA Rail Canada (check on busbud.com) and the German Flixbus, which entered the Canadian market in April 2022. Other bus companies operating locally are Canada Bus, Megabus, and Rider Express.

Most buses are comfortable, with air-conditioning, washrooms, reclining seats (though they do not go back as far as business class seats in a plane), and reading lights. You may bring your own food and drink on board to pass the hours more comfortably. The bus makes regular, though very short, stops at terminals where there are restaurants and lavatories. Certain express buses do nonstop trips between city destinations.

Car Pooling

Car pooling is legal in Canada as long as drivers don't make profits. Since Greyhound left Canada, car pooling has become an increasingly popular way to travel across the country. You can use the Poparide platform to find your ride and share the cost of travel with the driver and the other passengers. It's affordable, safe, and secure as both riders and drivers have verified profiles, contact e-mails and phone numbers, as well as credit cards and bank accounts. The mobile app is easy to use, and the platform boasts nearly a million subscribers who can offer or book their rides on it.

Trains

The railway system is extensive; with 31,070 miles (50,000 km) of tracks it is one of the largest in the world. However, it has lost much of its popularity with passengers because of the competition from cars, fast planes, and cheap long-distance buses. Today it is mainly used for freight transport, though quite a number of passengers still use certain routes, such as between Toronto, Ottawa, and Montreal. While the trains are not necessarily cheaper than flying, they do provide unique views, comfort, and good service.

The passenger rail service is primarily operated by VIA Rail, which offers special passes that are good for a number of days over a period of a month. Service is less frequent than it used to be, but on long trips trains, like the transcontinental The Canadian, which runs between Toronto and Vancouver in three days, have special sleeping compartments and diner cars. Another tip is the two-day trip aboard the Rocky Mountaineer, which takes you from Vancouver through Jasper and Banff and all the way to Calgary.

Planes

Internal flights within Canada used to be prohibitively expensive. With the emergence of several budget airlines they no longer cost a small fortune, but are still more expensive than budget city-hopper prices in Europe and in the USA.

Air Canada is the main national carrier, and there are several smaller airlines including Air Transat (based in Montreal), Air North (based in Yukon), and West Jet (based in Calgary, Alberta). Porter Airlines operates from Billy Bishop Airport, Toronto, with flights to other Canadian cities, US cities, and the Caribbean. Air travel in Canada is safe, clean, and a fast, efficient way to get to distant locations.

HEALTH AND SAFETY

Canada is, for the most part, a clean and safe country. Just use common sense, as you would anywhere in the world. If you are walking around at night, especially alone, you should stay in well-lit, well-frequented areas. Keep a close watch on personal belongings, and make sure that wallets, cell phones, and valuables are safely out of sight and out of reach of pickpockets. When in doubt about an area of a city, ask the locals. Big cities have neighborhoods that are best avoided.

Should visitors to Canada become sick, there are walk-in clinics where no appointment is needed, though you may need to wait before you can see a doctor. Medical care in Canada is expensive for those who are not insured, and it is sensible to take out travel insurance before leaving your home country. Visitors will probably be asked for insurance details before seeing a doctor. The clinics are of good quality and can be trusted to provide good first-line care. In a medical emergency, one can go to the emergency department of any hospital.

SUMMER HEALTH TIPS: BEAT THE BUGS

- Avoid nature parks in July.
- Stock up on anti-bug and anti-itch creams and sprays, and just accept the pesticides.
- Always have light-colored, lightweight, long-sleeved shirts and trousers and wear them from the moment the sun starts to set. This is not the time for those trendy shorts.
- Buy a hat with a mosquito net that pulls down to your shoulders.
- Use double-mesh screens on tents and cottages and always keep them closed (it's not for nothing that all Canadian houses are equipped with screens on doors and windows).
- Before leaving on your trip, look at the Web site theweathernetwork.com, which is an excellent site for weather information and has a bug report per city.

One particular hazard in Canada is extreme cold weather. Appropriate clothing is essential for a winter visit. Transportation, homes, offices, and shops are all well heated, but wearing the right clothes when out of doors will make your stay much more pleasant. If you are staying in hotels, the staff will indicate what conditions are like and what precautions to take. When traveling by car in the winter, it is advisable to have a blanket and a candle in the car in case of a breakdown.

It is a custom to open both the hood and the trunk of a car that breaks down, and to use the emergency lights. Passers-by will then call for help. If you have a cell phone, call for help immediately (the emergency number is 911 across the country, though a local traffic number may be indicated along the road) and, in the winter, stay in the car—the candle will keep you warm.

WINTER HEALTH TIPS: WRAP UP WARMLY

- Have a hat that covers your ears.
- Wear a long scarf that can cover your neck, mouth, and ears if necessary.
- You'll want gloves or mittens (mittens are warmer).
- Bring a warm coat, made for winter weather.
- You'll need winter boots (lined and waterproof) or rubber overshoes.
- It's advisable in winter to dress in layers that can be peeled off or hauled on as the scene changes: sweating indoors and freezing outside is a recipe for catching a cold. Wool is the warmest material, so do bring woolen sweaters, and woolen stockings are fashionable for women. Thin thermal underclothing is also available in Canada and is great for keeping you warm and dry.

CHAPTER EIGHT

BUSINESS BRIEFING

For many years, Canada has been recognized as one of the most business-friendly countries in the world. Government policies and administration are generally supportive, there is an independent and reliable judicial system, and financial structures are stable and efficient. In 2022 The Economist Intelligence Unit ranked Canada second out of 82 countries for its global business environment, and first among the G7.

The business visitor will generally be welcomed with open arms—Canada's economy is hugely trade-focused and contacts with foreign companies are not only common but actively sought after. Furthermore, the country's highly diverse workforce and its policies of cultural tolerance make for a pleasant and cooperative environment.

Culturally, doing business in Canada is similar to doing business in other Western industrialized countries, particularly the USA and the UK. However, as we have seen, there are particularities in the way that Canadians do things that are important to keep in mind. For a start, and it is worth repeating here, Canadians do not like to be taken for, treated as, or assumed to be like Americans. It is also important to remember that the information that follows is a general guideline and cannot fully reflect the huge variations between economic sectors, the regional and provincial differences, or the cultural diversity between companies.

THE WORK ETHIC

Canadians are hardworking. This is partly the result of the widespread respect for merit; a person's only path to success is through what he or she can achieve under his or her own steam. There is little favoritism in the business culture due to a fundamental belief in equal opportunities for everyone, regardless of social background, gender, or culture. Corruption levels are low, partly because there are rules and regulations that control it but also because Canadians have a strong sense of "doing the right thing."

The work ethic is reinforced by several external factors; Canadians work long hours, have very few holidays, and there is little job security. In order for Canada's economy to remain competitive in the current environment there is increasing pressure for the workforce to spend longer at the office. General business hours are from 9:00 a.m. to 5:00 p.m., from

Monday to Friday, though this does of course vary depending on the sector and type of company or organization. In the commercial and service sectors, even Sundays are now workdays in many parts of the country. Administrative staff may stick to the hours they are contracted for, but professionals and managers generally chalk up many more hours.

In terms of job conditions, the average holiday allowance for Canadians is twelve days a year. Only after around ten years of service in the same company may employees have as much as the average European four weeks off. Furthermore, compared to European norms, the private sector in Canada provides less job security. The 10 percent of the labor force who work for the government enjoy more generous conditions than workers in the private sector.

LABOR RELATIONS AND LEGISLATION

Labor relations and employment laws are divided between the federal and provincial governments. Federal authority covers interprovincial economic sectors such as communications, broadcasting, banking, and transportation. Everything else, including all manufacturing, the service industry, and health and education, is provincially regulated. Thirty percent of the Canadian workforce is unionized; Quebec has a higher incidence of unionization than other provinces. Most collective agreements are concluded between a union and an employer rather than across an industry or region. What is unique to the Canadian context is the "delay of work stoppage" ruling, which demands that before a strike can be called there are certain steps to be taken (such as a vote among members). This gives a cooling-off period for both sides in order to avoid work stoppages, and, in fact, 95 percent of collective agreements are negotiated without industrial action.

PROFESSIONALISM

Despite the need to work hard, there is generally a high degree of job satisfaction in the Canadian workforce. Culturally, Canadians tend to do as well as they can in their jobs and take pride in their accomplishments. This isn't to say that the work environment is perfect and that everyone is happy, but that, comparatively speaking, Canadians are not only hardworking—they like it that way. Maintaining a healthy work–life balance is not easy, but by dedicating what free time they do have available to family and friends, they generally seem to manage.

The Canadian workforce is highly qualified and well educated. This is in part due to the fact that the business sector has an important influence in technical training institutes and colleges on the subjects taught and how students are prepared for the labor market. Furthermore, immigration policies aim specifically to fill labor shortages.

Women are well respected at all levels of business and government, though not all the barriers and sexist attitudes have been eliminated. Women make up 54.4 percent of the workforce and fill 47.3 percent of managerial positions; visitors from very conservative countries should therefore be prepared to deal with women in the boardroom. Female business travelers to Canada can expect to be treated with respect and taken seriously.

THE OFFICE CULTURE

Canadians are respectful of authority, and this attitude is also reflected in the workplace. In Canadian business culture, rank is earned by personal achievement, and respect toward senior colleagues is expected. However, the workplace in Canada is generally collegial. Even in Quebec, the Quebecois are far less formal and hierarchical than the French in France. Across the country, managers are expected to lead by example. The leadership style is honest, team-oriented, and highly communicative, rather than directive. Decision-making processes follow a similar line. Mutual responsibility and transparency are important, as are cooperation and respecting professional responsibility. Decisions will be based on knowledge and facts, not on gut feelings.

Canadians at work are often described as conservative, which reflects the values of modesty and humility that we saw in Chapter 2. Loud, pompous, or aggressive communication styles are discouraged. As far as dressing for work goes, the latest fashions and flash are not particularly approved of. Clothing and dress style in Canada is not a sign of rank: appropriate dress will vary according to the sector, type of company, and the style of the particular organization. The owner of a factory, for instance, may wear a pair of jeans and have his sleeves rolled up. What is important is neatness and appropriateness of the attire. Visitors would do better to come overdressed on the first day of a visit rather than dress too casually. For most city-based companies, a dark business suit is a safe bet for both men (with a tie) and women (either skirt or slacks).

A final note: Canadian noses are sensitive. Offices will, for the most part, be nonsmoking. Perfume is not generally worn, but any scents or aftershaves should be light and subtle.

MEETINGS

First impressions are important. Always book meetings in advance, preferably a few days beforehand, but give longer notice if possible. Letters and phone calls should be succinct and polite. Being on time is important; if you are going to be late, Canadians probably won't wait more than fifteen minutes unless you call to inform them of the delay. It is seen as rude to be late in the business world, even in Quebec, where the Latin sense of time is a bit more flexible.

Both men and women shake hands at the beginning and often also at the end of business meetings. Men may wait for a woman to offer her hand first rather than initiating a handshake. Across the country, eye contact is important, as it is seen as friendly, open, and trusting behavior. Anglophone Canadians tend to use subdued body language; they do not touch and keep a distance between themselves in discussions. French Canadians, on the other hand, are more physically expressive and tend to observe less physical distance.

It is best to use titles, like Mr., Mrs., or Dr. during business meetings. In Quebec, it is best to use the formal *vous* ("you") until asked to switch to the informal *tu*. If people wish you to call them by their first name, they will say so. The business environment may appear more relaxed than in other countries, but it is always better to err on the side of formality and politeness than to be thought disrespectful.

It is also advisable to establish in advance whether French or English is the preferred language of communication. Even in Quebec it may be possible to speak in English in the corporate world, but it is important to ask in advance to avoid misunderstandings. In any part of Canada, if the company has French-language ties it is a good idea to have all printed materials, including business cards, promotional materials, and presentations, printed in French. This may seem an unnecessary added expense, but it will be highly appreciated. Also, using a few words of French at the beginning of a meeting will increase goodwill and probably get things started in a more relaxed atmosphere.

During meetings, the seating arrangement will be informal, except perhaps for the position of the highest-ranking person in the room. The business proceedings will start quickly. Meetings tend to be cooperative in nature; whereas clearly the boss will make the decisions for the company, discussions will be open, and each individual present will be able to contribute from his or her own perspective and expertise.

PRESENTATIONS

Canadian hosts will expect a visitor to come well prepared, to be knowledgeable, and to be ready to do business. An agenda, with the purpose and duration of the meeting, will have been established in advance, and will be kept to; discussions unrelated to work will be minimal. Whether you are making a presentation, negotiating, or just sharing information, Canadians will not be impressed by something that is simply a good show. They respect individuals who can back up their story with data and details. A straightforward and realistic presentation style will go over better than hype. You will be expected to be a good listener and have a flexible approach.

NEGOTIATING

The Canadians have the reputation of being among the most reasonable and pleasant people to negotiate with. They are goal-oriented and looking for the bottom line, but they do so in a way that seeks a win-win situation for all those around the table. They have little respect for the "hard sell" approach, or a "glitz and blitz" attitude to pushing a deal through.

Canadians place trust in contracts and lawyers; all aspects of a deal will be aboveboard and legally sound. However, they also place trust in people, which is why establishing good relations is important. While mutual respect is the basis of a good deal, it will not lead to favoritism. They value solid working relationships with partners, based on respect and cooperation. Because they place an emphasis on organization and pay attention to detail, their negotiating style appears cautious; their open and cooperative attitude tends to give the negotiation process an unhurried feel. Canadians are self-confident and direct, and value good listening skills in making deals.

Negotiations will end in a direct plan of action and a deal will be closed with drinks or a meal.

CONTRACTS

Contracts in Canada are binding and recognized by Canada's courts. They are governed by common law and statutes in all provinces and territories except for Quebec, where the Civil Code (originally based on the French Civil Code system) applies. This is unique in North America. The statutes, which apply to any given contract, will vary in each province and territory. These cover legally binding rules that cannot be contradicted by a contract. In labor law, for instance, these cover human rights, occupational health and safety, workers' compensation, and privacy regulations. In negotiating contracts, it would be wise to use the services of a local lawyer who is well informed on the specifics of the provincial legislation.

The Canadian attitude toward contracts is similar to that of the Americans. One tends to try to cover as many aspects of the deal as possible in the terms and agreements on paper. Once a contract is signed, you can be quite sure that your Canadian counterparts will follow the provisions in good faith.

BUSINESS LUNCHES

The business lunch is increasingly popular, though Canadians have traditionally not undertaken negotiations and serious business discussions over a meal. It is a time to get to know each other more informally. While being very friendly, Canadians will probably not share personal information with people they do not know well. Lunch will probably not last more than an hour and a half, and there is a strong likelihood that there will be no alcohol ordered by the Anglophone Canadians at the table. The Quebecois, on the other hand, are likely to order wine with their meal.

GIFTS

Giving gifts to Canadian associates is most appropriate once a deal is finalized. Private-sector employees can accept small gifts, such as a bottle of wine. Probably the most suitable present is something from home, which represents the place the visitor is from. A wrapped gift will be unwrapped immediately and the giver thanked. Substantial gifts and cash are out of the question. Employees will have to tell their employer about anything received, and sometimes the gifts are pooled, perhaps to be shared around among the staff at the end of the year.

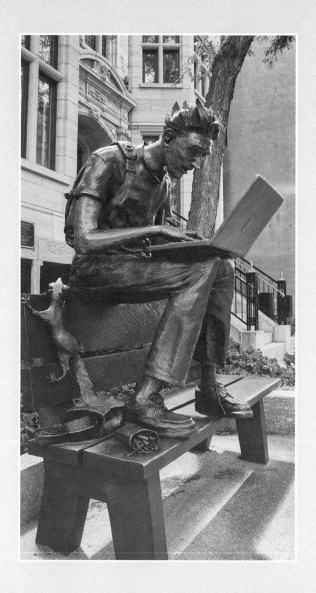

CHAPTER NINE

COMMUNICATING

LANGUAGE TICS

Canadian English sounds much like the English spoken in the northern American states. However, it would be a mistake to assume that the idioms are the same. Here are a few examples of some differences.

"Cold Out, Eh?"

Outside Canada, Canadians often have to endure a friendly rib-poking: "Oh, you're Canadian, EEEHHH?" (pronounced "ey" with an upward lilt). The chances are that this particular Canadian never said "eh" in his or her life, but the expression has become one of the best-known Canadian stereotypes. It was made famous by the comedians Rick Moranis and Dave Thomas as the McKenzie Brothers in their song ("Great White North"), TV skits, and movie (*Strange Brew*) in the 1970s and '80s. They wore thick, cotton plaid shirts and woolen tuques (the Canadian term for a knitted cap or beanie), and said "eh" a lot.

All right, maybe there is a tendency in some parts of Canada to use "eh," but it is the fact that it allows Canadians to turn statements into questions that is interesting. "Cold out, eh?" or "That was an awful show, eh?" Do Canadians do this as a polite way of seeking the opinion of others, or does it reflect a fear of putting their opinions out on a limb? Or is it simply a way of encouraging dialogue? Interpret it as you will, English-speaking Canadians often speak in questions.

"Sorry? Oh, Sorry. Sorry!"

Another little idiosyncrasy is the frequent use of the word "sorry," just as in England. We have seen that if someone steps on your foot, you say you are sorry (for having your foot in the wrong place). In this sense the word means "Oops, it's crowded in here." The word can also be used to mean "Pardon me," as in "Sorry, I didn't hear what you said", or "Excuse me" as in "Sorry, I would like to pass by you without being rude." It can be apologetic, as in "Sorry I stepped on your foot," but it can also be a way of expressing shock and horror, as in "I beg your pardon!" It's a handy word which, when combined with intonation and facial expressions, can be used subtly to express many emotions.

VOCABULARY

Canadian English is generally close to American English, though it retains strong influences from the British Isles. There are also influences from French (they would say "serviette" rather than "table napkin") and Native languages ("kayak" is Inuit, and many Algonquian words have entered the language, such as "moose," "skunk," "chipmunk," "raccoon," "squash," "moccasin," "woodchuck," and "toboggan"). There are regional expressions across all provinces and territories, many of which are influenced by immigrant groups or by geographical or local social realities. An example of this variety is the word for a rural vacation home: Western Canadians call it a cabin; Central and Eastern Canadians call it a cottage; Anglophones in Quebec call it a chalet; and those in New Brunswick call it a camp.

SOME CANADIANISMS

Allophone: A Canadian whose first language is neither French nor English

Canucks: Another word for Canadians, and the name of Vancouver's hockey team

Loonie: A one-dollar coin that pictures a loon (a bird with a wistful call)

Parkade: A parking garage, to most Western Canadians

Toonie: A two-dollar coin

Skidoo: A snowmobile

Duplex: Two houses under one roof

Humongous: Something very, very big

In terms of pronunciation, there are a few particularities, such as the pronunciation of the "ou" sound. For instance, "about" sometimes sounds like "aboot." But generally Canadian English is easy to understand for both native and non-native English-speakers.

Not Bad Words in Canada

To do dick, or dick all, means to do nothing, to hang around.

Homo milk is homogenized milk.

To be pissed is to be drunk.

To be pissed off is to be annoyed. (Also used by Americans, this expression is not considered to be vulgar, as it is in Britain.)

A suck is a whiner, or crybaby.

Spelling

Canadian English uses a mix of British and American spelling. Some of the British English spelling stems from French, which would seem to be a good reason to prefer it—a sort of literary support of Canada's bilingual identity. But no official spelling site or dictionary gives this as a reason for the eclectic mix. Another reason for the spelling preferences may be that it reflects the Canadian "I'm not American" identity. Whatever the historic, emotional, or cultural reason, they retain the "u" in words like "colour" and "neighbour," and "re" in words like "centre" and "theatre." They also use two spellings of words where it is convenient: for instance, a cheque is a form of payment, while a check is a tick ($\sqrt{}$) or a verb meaning "to verify." It may be a good idea to consult a Canadian dictionary!

Canadian French

Canadian French is as different from the French spoken in France as standard British English is from Texan English. Not only are the accents poles apart, but the vocabulary used is also different. Quebecois is rooted in sixteenth- and seventeenth-century France. It was influenced by native languages and more recently also by English. It has a picturesque vocabulary, which uses visual imagery that reflects the geography and history of its people. For instance, in France, the expression used to describe the idea that someone has not seen the end of their troubles is *Il n'est pas sorti de l'auberge* (he hasn't yet made it out of the inn). In Quebec, the expression is *Il n'est pas sorti du bois* (he hasn't yet made it out of the forest), reflecting the fact that getting lost in a Canadian forest is far more likely, and more difficult to get out of, than a hotel.

Old expressions and words have been kept in Quebec that were long ago dropped in France. In Quebec, to lock a door is *barrer une porte*, which harks back to the time when a large wooden bar was placed across a door to secure it from the inside. In

France they prefer to *fermer à clef*, which is "to close with a key" (a more modern version of the same thing).

While some words are derived from English, many other terms were "Frenchified" when in France the English word was adopted. A rocking chair in Quebec is a *chaise berçante* (a chair that rocks), whereas it is a *rocking* in France. A puzzle is a *casse-tête* (a head breaker) in Quebec and a *puzzle* in France. The Quebecois have also invented words for recent inventions where only English words exist: the French use the English word "*émail*" whereas the Quebecois have invented the word *courriel*, which stands for *courrier electronique* (electronic mail).

In other cases English words have been totally adopted in Quebec where perfectly good French words exist: *charier* comes from the word "to carry," *rusher* is a verb which means to rush about, and *beurre de pinottes* is literally "butter of peanuts."

For many years Quebecois was seen as an underclass accent. The Quebecois spoken today in Quebec has gained national and international acceptance as a colorful and expressive accent. Quebec's active role in the International Organization of La Francophonie as well as the popularity of Quebec's artists in France have even permitted some Quebecois words and expressions to enter mainstream French in France.

A FEW HANDY WORDS FOR ANGLOPHONE VISITORS	
Dépanneur	Corner store
Metro	Subway
Autoroute	Highway
Liqueur	Soda pop (like Coke)
Arrêt	A stop sign meaning STOP
Guichet automatic	ATM machine
Condo	A condominium

THE MEDIA

One of the elements that bind the Canadian nation together is the media. It allows people from the various regions to communicate with each other, share a Canadian perspective, and develop cultural ties. The influence of television and radio in this sense cannot be underestimated. Canada's media networks are as modern as they come; its newspapers, television networks, and Internet connections are well developed and highly efficient.

Newspapers

There are two national papers in Canada, *The Globe and Mail* and the *National Post*, and each major city has one or two local daily papers. There are also several French-language papers, including *La Presse* and *Le Devoir*. There is, however, an ongoing debate about the increasing concentration of newspaper ownership.

In 2022, seventy-six newspapers in Canada were owned by large conglomerates, approximately half of which belonged to Postmedia Network Inc./Sun Media. The second-largest ownership group, Torstar Media, had seven. Independents accounted for six other newspapers. There has been concern about the loss of variety of perspectives in Canadian papers, and the ability of the press to play the critical social role expected of the media in a democracy.

Ownership legislation lags behind many European countries. This is partly because the industry itself claims that, without this concentration, Canadian

papers could not survive because of the small size of the Canadian market. While there are independent newspapers in several cities, recent reports have pointed to extreme concentrations in the provinces of Saskatchewan, New Brunswick, Prince Edward Island, and Newfoundland and Labrador. Furthermore, journalists are finding it increasingly difficult to produce in-depth articles of quality because of budget cuts within the large corporations.

Canada's largest online news site is thestar.com. It ranges from national coverage and issues to local headlines and stories across the country.

For foreign visitors anxious to keep up with news from home, international papers are available in a limited number of outlets in the major urban centers.

Television and Radio

Canadians are enthusiastic consumers of both television and radio programs. The biggest issue in programming is Canada's proximity to the US market, which pumps massive amounts of American content into Canadian homes. Successive Canadian governments have understood that without support the production of Canadian content would not be able to compete with American programming, and Canadian content would dwindle. In order to ensure both the expression and consumption of Canadian culture, the government takes the following three-pronged approach.

Government-owned broadcasters provide significant amounts of Canadian content and thus support the expression of Canadian culture. The Canadian Broadcasting Corporation (CBC) and the Société de Radio-Television du Canada (SRC) show 60 percent Canadian content per day, and around 90 percent during prime time.

Laws and regulations ensure that all other Canadian providers air minimum amounts of Canadian content per day. In television this is generally 60 percent over their daily programming and 50 percent during prime time.

Federal and provincial governments also provide a variety of grants, subsidies, loans, and tax incentives to encourage the production of Canadian content.

In terms of television providers, there are several networks as well as cable and satellite providers. There are four nationwide networks: the CBC and the SRC, the Canadian Television Network (CTV), and Global/CanWest. In addition to these, there are also forty regional networks, several provincial government-supported networks, and local stations, as well as several commercial networks. Many American stations are available on the regular network service.

There is no TV license required in Canada, so networks (even government broadcasters) compete for advertising for their income. Thus the number of commercials on Canadian television approaches the level of the USA, which can be very irritating to European viewers. Much of the Canadian content tries to compete with American popular shows and some Canadian-made sitcoms are imitations of American ones. There are, however, also some popular shows that are enjoyed by Canadians across the country. Quebec produces a large amount of French-language content and has a broad and active arts and entertainment sector that accounts for much Canadian content. Programs from France and translations of American and European shows account for the rest.

The biggest difference between American and Canadian television and radio is the quality of the news broadcasts, in both French and English. The CBC takes its cue from the BBC and produces good quality programs that provide a mix of national and international stories.

Note that the television and video standard in Canada is NTSC, the same as in the USA. Foreign-bought televisions will not work in Canada, and videos bought in Canada will not work elsewhere.

USEFUL WEB SITES FOR NATIONAL AND INTERNATIONAL NEWS

www.theweathernetwork.com
The Weather Network is a Canadian English-language weather information specialty channel.

www.globalnews.ca
Global News is the news and current affairs division of the Canadian Global Television Network.

www.cbc.ca
CBC.ca is the English-language online service of the Canadian Broadcasting Corporation. It was introduced in 1996.

Red Canada Post mailboxes with an anti-graffiti design.

SERVICES

Mail

The Canadian postal service is reliable but not very fast. By European standards it is quite slow. There are options for sending domestic mail that are quicker but more expensive: Priority Post guarantees next day delivery, and Xpresspost guarantees delivery within two days. Canada Post is the national carrier, but there are also a few private companies and flourishing courier companies, which are more expensive but more practical when time is of the essence.

Post offices are usually open from 10:00 a.m. to 5:00 p.m., Mondays to Fridays, though this varies greatly from place to place. Some close at lunchtime, some are open for a few hours on Saturdays. Urban offices will have longer operating hours than rural ones.

Telephone and Internet

Canadians are enthusiastic telephone users. Practically everyone owns at least one landline, for which there is a flat rate per month, and all local calls are free. In 2022 the number of smartphone owners in Canada reached 32.3 million, or 85 percent of the population, though the service is still relatively expensive. A note of caution with cell phones: some rural areas have no coverage at all, and some providers do not cover the whole country. Also, cell phones from outside the country may not work in Canada because of differences in band frequencies. There is now a plethora of phone companies and mobile service providers who compete for business. Rates vary, particularly on the cost of international calls. This is why apps like WhatsApp, Messenger, or Fongo are very useful to have.

Internet access and use is also widespread; at least 70 percent of all adults go online regularly. While fax machines may still be used by doctors and pharmacists, e-mail has become the norm for both business and personal communication.

CONCLUSION

So what is there to know about Canadian culture? The country is peaceful and everything works; the people are friendly and honest, easy to understand, and very polite.

Culture Smart! Canada shows that Canadian culture is far more complex than the stereotypes would lead us to believe. Certain stereotypes don't add up: Canadians are not bilingual, their population speaks many languages; Canadians are not more environmentally friendly than other Western industrialized peoples—the impact of their lifestyle is diluted by the size of their country.

The biggest intercultural mistake a visitor can make is to assume that the Canadians are like the Americans. Their history, international reputation, culture, and self-image are in part based on not being American: Canada is not a superpower but is internationally respected as a bastion of moderation and good sense; Canadians are not united by one national identity but are a mosaic of distinct cultural identities. While they are proud of their international reputation, they are more loyal to their province or community than to their nation.

This book attempts to describe the Canadians as they see themselves. The Quebecois, for instance, rarely get a chance to display their point of view to an English-speaking audience. Here, you may discover that many famous actors and musicians are Canadian, though many assume that they are American. Canada is a hip, progressive, and liberal country that is at the forefront of many social developments, such as multiculturalism and progressive education systems.

For the visitor, Canadians are hospitable and easy to get to know; they are among the most reasonable people in the world to do business with, and they are fun to be around during moments of leisure. Here's wishing you a pleasant journey. *Bon voyage!*

USEFUL APPS

Communication

iTranslate
If you're in Quebec and your French is rusty, this language app can translate text, voice, and images.

Canadians are avid social media users. Their favorite apps in order of poularity are **Facebook**, **TikTok**, **Twitter**, **Instagram**, and **Reddit**.

Travel and Transportation

AllTrails
Packed with 100,000 hiking paths and mountain bike routes, this app makes it easy to discover new trails in parks across Canada.

blogTO
Toronto event listings, restaurant reviews, news, and current affairs.

Flush
A toilet finder app that includes info on accessibility.

Gasbuddy
Find the cheapest gas stations nearby.

Google Maps
Route plan and view public transit timetables.

Hotels.com
Make reservations for anywhere, any price range, and for any length of time.

Lyft
Versatile app for ride-hailing, as well as vehicle hire, motorized scooters, and bicycle-sharing in cities in Vancouver and various Ontario cities.

Roadtrippers (Canada)
A powerful route planner showing some well-kept secrets, beauty spots, road attractions, national parks, and surprise stops for the adventurous traveler.

Transit App
Get real time public transit information; including routes, timetables, and tracking.

Uber
Hail a ride in cities country-wide.

Food and Shopping

Amazon.ca is Canada's most popular online shopping platform, followed by **Walmart.ca** and **Well.ca**.

DoorDash
Food delivery service that offers monthly subscription service for free deliveries.

Foupon Groupon
Canada's most popular deal app, from restaurants to spas, shopping, travel, etc.

GrubHub
Popular food delivery app for Ontario.

SkipTheDishes
Canada's largest food delivery service from local restaurants.

Tim Hortons
Delivery of food and drinks offered by Canada's most popular coffee chain.

UberEats
Food delivery from local restaurants, including local breweries. Available in most major cities country-wide.

USEFUL WEB SITES

Canada.gc.ca
Government of Canada's main portal

pch.gc.ca
Official Canadian Heritage Site

1000towns.ca
Plan your trip by exploring what Canada's different towns have to offer

thecanadaguide.com
Online resource for Canadian history, society, and culture

movingtocanada.com
Comprehensive resource for... you guessed it

jobbank.gc.ca/findajob
Want to look for a job in Canada? Start here

cbc.ca
For Canadian news and current affairs

statcan.gc.ca
Multimedia site of Statistics Canada

FURTHER READING

Adams, Michael. *Fire and Ice: The United States, Canada and the Myth of Converging Values*. Toronto: Penguin Canada, 2009 (paperback).

Bédard, Éric. *L'histoire du Québec pour les nuls*. Paris: First Éditions, 2019.

Brown, Jesse *et al. The Canadaland Guide to Canada*. New York: Touchstone, 2017.

Casselman, Bill. *Casselmania: More Wacky Canadian Words and Sayings*. Toronto: McArthur and Company, 1999.

Chartier, Daniel. *Le guide de la culture au Québec: Litérature, cinéma, essays, revues*. Quebec City: Éditions Nota bene, 2004.

Coupland, Douglas. *Souvenir of Canada*. Madeira Park, BC: Douglas and McIntyre (2013) Ltd.

Doughty, Howard A., and Marino Tuzi (eds.). *Discourse and Community: Multidisciplinary Studies of Canadian Culture*. Toronto: Guernica Editions, 2007.

Esrock, Robin. *The Great Canadian Bucket List*. Toronto: Dundurn Press, 2nd ed. 2017.

Field, Luke Gordon and Alex Huntley. *The Beaverton Presents Glorious and/or Free: The True History of Canada*. Toronto: Penguin Canada, 2017.

Ferguson, Will, and Ian Ferguson. *How to be a Canadian*. Vancouver: Douglas & McIntyre, 2008.

Grescoe, Taras. *Sacré Blues: An Unsentimental Journey through Quebec*. Toronto: MacFarlane Walter & Ross, 2001: Westminster, Maryland, USA: McClelland & Stewart Ltd., 2001.

Hayday, Matthew and Raymond B. Blake, eds. *Celebrating Canada, Volume 1: Holidays, National Days, and the Crafting of Identities*. Toronto: University of Toronto Press, 2016.

Heath, Joseph. *The Efficient Society: Why Canada is as Close to Utopia as it Gets*. Toronto: Penguin Global, paperback 2005.

King, Thomas. *The Incovenient Indians: A Curious Account of Native People in North America*. Toronto: Doubleday Canada, 2012; Minneapolis: University of Minnesota Press 2018.

Riendeau, Roger E. *A Brief History of Canada*. Markham, Ontario: Fitzhenry & Whiteside, 2000; NY: Facts on File, 2007.

Cover image: *Train passing through the Bow River valley against the backdrop of the Rockies.* © Shutterstock by Tomas Kulaja.

INDEX